TEENER BASEBALL

Gregory L. Heitmann

Copyright © 2010 Gregory L. Heitmann

All rights reserved.

ISBN-10: 0615819265
ISBN-13: 9780615819266 (Gregory L. Heitmann)

Teener Baseball

Gregory L. Heitmann

Dedicated to the great people of South Dakota.

Gregory L. Heitmann

Many thanks to my family, gracias!

Special thanks to my brother, Garrett.

As always, a big thank you to my editors:

Angela

Dorene

Gwyneth

Gregory L. Heitmann

Author's Note

This is a work of fiction and the usual rules apply. The characters, the conversations, and the incidents portrayed in this novel have been invented by the author. Nothing in this book is to be construed as real. Any resemblance to actual events, or persons, whether living or dead, is coincidental. Again, none of the characters are real. Although Teeners is an actual baseball league in South Dakota, and I did play baseball, this is a fictional story conceived for entertainment purposes only and is not to be construed as a historical volume.

Gregory L. Heitmann

Other novels by Gregory L. Heitmann:

Fort Sisseton – Dakota Territory

Chief Red Iron – The Lakota Uprising

The G MANN 2 – Pay-2-Play

Gregory L. Heitmann

What people are saying about "Teener Baseball"

-

"This book is completely misogynistic!"
-Some Woman

"If I would have known this is what baseball would become, I would never have let people say I invented it."
-Abner Doubleday

"Lewd, crude, and vulgar...I loved it!"
-Greg's mom

"Hilariously gross and outrageous!"
-Anonymous

Gregory L. Heitmann

Chapter 1
Batter Up!

People familiar with the small towns of the Midwest can easily connect with America's past time. To be clear, I am talking about baseball; I'm not sure if anyone actually refers to baseball as a "past time" anymore, so the nostalgia of baseball is the impetus of this tale. The game of baseball is a dominating summer activity for youth in these small towns that dot the farming communities in the breadbasket of America. Boys and girls alike partake in the ritual of chasing 'round the bases, putting bat to ball, and playing catch. Now the category of "small town" is a relative term; however, for edification, and for the purposes of this story, "small town" is a community with a population between 300 and 3,000. Population numbers are a little arbitrary, but, to put a finer point on it, these villages are the ones that feature a skyscraper-esque building or multiple buildings that are also known as grain elevators.

Smaller kids, ages five and six years, old begin learning the game through the town's Pee Wee League baseball. The next level is Midget baseball, affectionately known as Midgets. Not quite the politically correct term nowadays, but it was a defining rite of passage moving from Pee Wees to Midgets; no more hitting a baseball off a "T." Midgets moved a child away from any games that include setting a ball on a stand to hit it. No, no T-ball. In Midgets the players pitched and hit. The youth baseball league was a convenient morning babysitter for many parents. Practices were conducted by a couple of boys home from college, hired by the city, and making a little money for tuition while they worked on the family farm or played a little amateur baseball themselves. The minds of the baseball playing youngsters were indelibly stamped with their assigned team names taken from the likes of the Dodgers, Yankees, Cardinals, Cubs, and even the Twins. Subconsciously, many of these kids, now adults, will have an inclination to look at box scores of "their" teams in the sports pages.

Here on the "mean" streets of these villages and burgs, these kids learned the value of teamwork and competition. It was a time before trophies were handed out for "participation;" you actually earned a trophy in Pee Wees or Midgets. Rivers of tears were shed learning the lessons of winning and losing, but valuable lessons they were. Baseball players and good citizens graduated to the next level of society from these little leagues. Alas, gone are the days when a child might have to actually succeed to be rewarded. The trophy industry now thrives as modern society considers everyone a winner…here's your trophy. Little did we know the importance of competition and encouraging excellence in the simple ways of yesteryear by rewarding winning and not just any behavior. I will jump down off my soap box now; after all, this is a story about baseball, not a sociological profile, or is it? I guess you can be the judge of that.

Chapter 2
Little League

1975 - Hutton, South Dakota

    The familiar Midwestern town skyline includes two key ingredients: a water tower and a grain elevator. Hutton, South Dakota, population 2,117 had them both. In fact Hutton has two grain elevators. The rich farmland of the surrounding area has been plowed from its native prairie a hundred or so years ago and is now producing grain at alarming rates.

    Overhanging the beautiful, wide, and kempt curb and gutter streets are giant elms, ash, and cottonwood trees. These trees are at the peak of their lives. Nestled in the urban forest are the residential areas of the citizens' varied styles of homes. Colonial, brick, ranch, split-level, bungalow, a myriad of architectural styles line the proud streets woven together by a common denominator...manicured lawns. If you are someone of status in this town, you have a lawn like Augusta National, the home of the Masters Golf Tournament.

    The sun shines through the greenery overhead, splashing shadows over a chubby young twelve-year old boy riding his bike as two other children on bicycles approach from behind, racing down the bucolic street setting. Their legs pump furiously, attempting to gain ground on the happy-go-lucky lad. Plump Bobby Jim Booth is oblivious to his surroundings. Clad in his baseball uniform, baseball glove hanging from his handlebars, he enjoys the leisurely ride home. With twenty-five extra pounds on his frame, Bobby Jim exerts an effort to propel his bike, made more complicated by the fact that he carries his favorite baseball bat in one hand, steering only with his single, free hand. The Midget game is done for the day, and Bobby is homeward bound when he hears a familiar voice call to him, "B.J., wait up!"

    Alex Chambers, also twelve years old and wearing his baseball uniform, calls out again from a distance, "B.J.!"

    Bobby Jim coasts to a stop and sticks his feet out as he turns his bike to face Alex. Alex is accompanied by eleven-year old Janet Rollins. Janet is a star on the Midget baseball team, and Bobby smiles broadly when he sees her in her baseball uniform, gliding on her bike toward him.

"Hi, guys. What do you want?" Bobby Jim smiles innocently as he looks first to Alex, then fixes his eyes on his crush. He is distracted by the cute girl that has followed him on his way home.

Alex and Janet lay on the brakes of their bikes and skid to a stop next to Bobby. Alex glowers at Bobby, "Nothing much…"

Alex and Janet straddle their bikes. Bobby looks quizzically back and forth between the two; his smile turns to a frown. He knows what's next.

Alex growls, "Just don't bother comin' to the games anymore, would ya?"

"Yeah," Janet chimes in. "We might actually win a game without your four strikeouts and eight errors every day!"

Bobby shrugs, "I guess I'll think about it."

Bobby turns his wheel towards home and struggles to get moving. He inches forward, clawing at the pedals with his feet. The handlebars flail wildly in his attempt to get moving while struggling with one hand on his bat and one on the handlebar. He is used to the harsh words. "Just ignore them," that's what his mom always says.

Alex is off his bike, throwing it to the ground with a crash. Bobby looks over his shoulder at the sound of the crashing bike. This was new to him, Alex chasing him down. The pursuit was short. Alex grabs Bobby's handlebar and halts the bike with a jolt. "You'll do more than think about it!" Alex hisses, shoving his face within an inch of Bobby's.

Bobby notices the fuzz on Alex's face when the sun pierces the canopy of the leaves rustling overhead. For the first time he notices that Alex looks much older, almost manly, with his face contorted in anger. Alex continues his rant, "We don't want you on our team! Stop coming to the games! You are making us lose!"

Bobby is distracted by the thoughts rattling through his head regarding this strange awareness of Alex and his age. He doesn't respond to Alex. Infuriated by Bobby's lack of response, Alex curls his hand into a small fist. He waves it threateningly under Bobby's nose.

Janet rides forward on her bike, "That's enough, Alex. He gets the picture."

Alex doesn't move. Through gritted teeth, Alex growls again slowly, "Do we understand each other?"

Bobby is very still. He stares at his aggressor; finally breaking eye contact with Alex, he glances bewilderedly at Janet. He answers stuttering, "I-I-I love baseball. Nothing will stop me from playing."

"Oh, yeah?" Alex cocks his head, bringing his balled up fist back to his ear.

His fist moves quickly, popping Bobby in the nose. It is not a brutal punch, but a cat-like jab. Blood trickles from Bobby's nose. Equal shares from the pain and the astonishment that Alex has hit him overwhelm Bobby. The blow to the nose makes his eyes water, he loses his balance, and he tumbles down to the pavement, folding into his bike, trapped like a prisoner in stocks.

Alex walks to his bike and hoists it to its wheels. He points to Bobby with an accusing finger, "I don't want to see you around the baseball field anymore!"

Janet catches Bobby's eye. Her stunned look says it all. She skips forward, pushing her bike and pedaling after Alex, leaving Bobby in a heap on the empty street.

Wriggling free from the bike that has fallen and become a prison, Bobby fights back tears. He walks his bike and silently cries to himself. The only evidence of his inner pain are the tears streaming over his cheeks.

* * *

Tossing his bike down in the driveway upon his arrival home, Bobby enters the split level house. He moves through the house to find his mother parked in her usual position, in front of the sink, washing dishes. Barbara Booth senses her son's presence in the kitchen. She doesn't turn as she concentrates her efforts on the suds and flatware, "Hi, Honey. How was your game?"

Silverware clanks against plates as she continues her chore. No answer from her son prompts the woman to look over her shoulder. She immediately sees the puffy eye and the dried blood surrounding Bobby's nostril. She wipes her hands quickly, not breaking eye contact with Bobby. She can see her son's physical and mental anguish in his eyes. Mrs. Booth moves to the refrigerator and takes out the ice tray from the freezer compartment. She places the ice in a towel and twists it into a ball in a smooth motion as she kneels in front of her boy, placing the ice pack on his eye and nose. "Did another ground ball get you? Come here."

His mother gently presses the cooling rag to Bobby's face as she pulls him in for a hug. Bobby's shoulders quiver and heave as he sobs into his mom's warm and flowery-scented shoulder.

Gregory L. Heitmann

"It was 1989,
My thoughts were short,
My hair was long.
Caught somewhere,
Between a boy and man."

    -Lyric from *All Summer Long* by Kid Rock

Gregory L. Heitmann

Chapter 3
Reedville

1989 – Reedville, South Dakota

As you travel the Yellowstone Trail east to west, Reedville, South Dakota, is on the way. The highway sign indicating U.S. 112 shares a placard also marking your path as part of the Old West Trail. The blue background with a white bison head bearing black letters announcing "Old West Trail" is a fine representation for a route marker, although the bison head sporting horns and a little beard can be easily confused with the head of a devil. The Yellowstone Trail has its own simple black and yellow sign bearing an arrow to assure tourists that they indeed are headed to Yellowstone National Park. The city entrance sign, the green sign with white lettering sporting "REEDVILLE" and smaller letters beneath, "POP. 1311," announces you are in Reedville.

These signs on the outskirts of Reedville compete heartily with a billboard denoting the state high school championships earned by the teams over the years. The board lists a myriad of sporting accolades ranging from track and field, basketball, football and even volleyball and gymnastics, but baseball honors dominate the sign, plastering about two-thirds of the board. The majority of the billboard exclaims: "Home of South Dakota State 'B' Teener Baseball Champs! 1980, 1981, 1982, 1983, 1984, 1986." Sharing equal billing is the Legion Baseball team, sporting its own championships about every other year since 1975. Baseball roots and successes run deep in Reedville. There is no more room for touting championships. The billboard would need to be widened to display additional information.

A quick turn down Main Street will take you to the central business district. At the south end of town, north of the grain elevators, you find the hub of commerce for the community. There is a grocery store, a drug store, a bowling alley, and a hardware store, the staples of every small farming community. Tucked in between the businesses are the American Legion Hall and the Veterans of Foreign Wars buildings. These are affectionately known as the Legion and the VFW. Both these organizations cater to the veterans of the military and are leaders in community service. Most notably, the Legion sponsors Legion baseball for boys seventeen to eighteen years old; the VFW sponsors Teener Baseball for boys fourteen to sixteen years old. Nearly every community in South Dakota, through their Legion and VFW, participates in this summer baseball program. Reedville happens to be very good at it. Their pipeline to baseball success starts at the Pee Wee level, then to Midget baseball, on to Teeners, and finally Legion baseball. Baseball is not part of high school sports. Many other states include baseball as a sanctioned high school activity, but not South Dakota in the 1980's

The north to south crossroad for Reedville is South Dakota State Highway 137. It intersects with U.S. 112, and this is the location of the closest thing to a traffic signal in the town. The traffic control device is a flashing yellow beacon for the eastbound and westbound traffic of U.S. 112. For the north and south traffic of Highway 37 it flashes a red beacon to assist the recognition of the stop condition and stop signs. This is a warning to drivers from both directions of the congestion, a relative term.

The quadrants of the intersection are dotted with a Ford car dealership, a Mobil gas station, a Dairy Queen, and the generic Kwik-Mart gas station. Traveling south down State Highway 137 from this intersection you are on the west side of Reedville, and here is where you find the baseball diamonds and softball fields of various sizes.

Even from quite a fair distance you can hear the sound of a baseball on a metal bat, the ringing clank followed by cheers rise from the Reedville Baseball Park. Not as traditional as the crack of bat when horsehide meets wood, the metal clank could be the trademarked sound of the Reedville baseball machine. A sound more likened to heavy industry, the clanking metal bat on ball is the product of the Reedville baseball machine.

Chapter 4
Game One

Tonight is the first game of the season. This evening's matchup features the Reedville Teeners against the neighboring town of Clarkston. In the dugout head coach Marvin Willis stands up from the bench and claps his hands. The loudspeaker crackles and the clear voice of a young lady announces the batter, "Now batting for Clarkston, centerfielder, Whitney White."

From the dugout Coach Willis claps again and barks out to the players in the field, "Come on, fellas! Show some life out there! Let's hear some chatter!"

Coach Willis is the sixty-five year old head coach for the Teener baseball team. He paces the dugout with a limp before sitting on the bench. He reaches for his right leg and bends the leg backwards at the knee; his grotesquely twisted leg is placed in his lap as he reties his shoe. Coach looks up from his shoe-tying task and yells, "Ok, Trent, keep throwing strikes!"

Coach Willis looks down the bench with a grin at his assistant coach, "One thing about losin' my leg to diabetes, it's easy to tie this here shoe."

Coach readjusts his prosthetic leg on its stump just below the knee. He sports the same uniform his players wear. His uniform shows the pounds, as it is for most aging men. Coach Willis spits some tobacco, and a little strained drool escapes the corner of his mouth. "Fire strikes, Trent!" Coach barks out.

On the field the Reedville Teeners provide chatter of support for their pitcher, "Come on, Trent!" Encouragement rains down from the right side of the infield.

"No batter!" shouts the left side of the infield.

Trent rocks and fires the ball to the plate, the ping of the baseball off a metal bat rings out a solid hit to the left side of the infield, the ball skipping between the shortstop and the third baseman. Members of the team in the dugout snap their heads to follow the ball to the outfield. Gary Hillmann, the Reedville left fielder, charges the ball, but doesn't get his glove down in the grass deep enough, and the ball scoots by him. He turns and runs to retrieve the ball, but two base runners score.

Groans emanate from the dugout. Assistant Coach Bobby Jim Booth stands and moves to the dugout steps closest to left field. He glares to the outfield, "Gary! What are you doing out there?"

"Take it easy, Boots," Coach Willis drawls.

Boots or Bootsy are a couple nicknames Bobby Jim Booth has picked up over the years since relocating to Reedville from Hutton. He is now a twenty-six year old teacher at Reedville High. Teaching is a perfect profession for Bobby as it provides the summers free to coach baseball and play a little amateur baseball himself.

"Well, Jesus Christ," Coach Boots turns to Coach Wills, "our best player can't even field a simple ground ball."

"Relax. It's our first game. There's bound to be a little rust on things."

Coach Boots flops his athletic frame back on the bench. He folds his arms, shakes his head, and heaves a big sigh. Coach Willis turns his attention from his young and impatient protégé back to the action on the field. With a bellowing voice, Coach calls from the dugout, "Shake it off now, Trent. Hummm, Babe. Just keep throwing strikes. Hey! Let's hear some chatter out there!"

Coach Boots calls out support to his pitcher. Bootsy wears his uniform well. He's in the best shape of his life, coming into his own season as the first string catcher for the Reedville amateur baseball team. Bobby stands and leans against the rail as Trent winds and fires. A ground ball to the second baseman is gobbled up, flipped to the shortstop, who touches second base, and submarine style tosses the ball to the first baseman ending the inning. A cheer goes up from the crowd echoed by Bootsy, "That a way to roll two, Trent."

With the side retired the Reedville fielders hustle off the field to the dugout. Coach Boots has his eye on Gary and steps to the entrance of the dugout cutting him off as Gary tries to stow his glove and cap while getting his batting gear. "What are you doing out there?" Bootsy whines a question.

"What?" Gary replies not giving his full attention as he tries to maneuver around the coach blocking his path.

"That ground ball? You let two runs in on that stupid play!"

Gary weaves one way, then back to the other, trying get to his gear. Bootsy grabs Gary by the shoulder, "Listen to me. I'm talking to you!"

Gary meets Coach Boots' eyes, "Uh, Coach, I'm trying to get my batting gloves here. I'm up third…"

Coach Bootsy's face begins to redden, framed by his thick, dark hair spilling from under his hat as he cuts Gary off mid-sentence, "…And I'm asking you a question! What the hell were you doing out there on the ground ball?"

Coach Boots and his large six-foot two frame looms over Gary, ten years his junior. Gary shrugs, "Well, the grass is pretty tall and thick. I just missed it. I didn't get my glove down."

Gary stares quizzically at Coach Boots. Coach Bootsy points at Gary. The coach's mouth moves, but no words come out as he fumes. He finally moves nose-to-nose with Gary, but Gary doesn't back down.

Coach Boots finally is able to conjure up a vocal response that is nothing more than a noise. "Rahhhhhhh!" bursts out of the man's mouth, emanating from his diaphragm, as his arms begin to flail, causing Gary to step back.

The growling noise catches Coach Willis' attention, "Jesus, Bobby! Relax! Get over to your coaching box." Coach Willis orders.

Boots stares at Gary a bit longer before finally jogging over to the first base coach's box. With Bootsy out of the way, Gary moves to the bench. He reties his shoes and adjusts his stockings. Gary Hillmann is the all-American sixteen year old boy. He is a good looking kid, brown hair, athletic build, smart, and charming. He has everything you need to be noticed and make it to the next level. He digs through his duffle bag and produces a pair of leather batting gloves and begins to put them on.

Dave Brown, Gary's best friend, shuffles over to him and plops down. Dave is still in all his catcher's equipment. "What was that about?" Dave asks.

Dave smiles in his typical jovial mood. He is a husky boy with a round freckled face and sandy hair. He is a large target, a good-sized backstop that makes for a quality catcher, his light batting skills aside. Sweat streams from his hairline down his face, as usual, from even the mildest exertion.

Gary shakes his head from side to side, "I have no idea, and I really don't care."

Dave gives a snort, "I wonder what got up Bootsy's butt?"

Gary shrugs and stands, donning his helmet and grabbing his bat. He holds out his hand in front of Dave and is slapped five by his friend. He heads up the steps of the dugout, and Dave calls to him, "Let's get those runs back."

Gary looks over his shoulder and gives a wink before turning his attention to the hitter already at the plate, "Come on, Trent! Start us off with a hit, Buddy!"

Trent Thompson is pitcher for this game and also the leadoff hitter. He is sixteen years old and quite athletic. He has been a starter for the varsity football and basketball teams since he was a freshman. He sports blonde-blonde hair and matching peach fuzz whiskers. He steps to the plate and promptly rips a single up the middle. The rout is on. The hits come from up and down the Reedville lineup. The two runs given up in the top of the first inning are more than made up for with a ten run outburst in the home team's bottom half of the inning. It is a short game as the ten-run rule is called, and the late evening turns to dark. The ten-run rule in Teener Baseball is a mercy rule. It shortens the game by declaring the game over when after the fifth inning, or other agreed upon inning, that if one of the teams is ahead by more than ten runs, the game is over. And the team with the ten run lead is awarded the victory. It is a way to shorten sometimes lengthy, one-sided games. A fifteen run rule after three innings is also sometimes in play to bring a sporting end to games dominated by one team.

Chapter 5
Let's Play Two

Towering lights hum to life, illuminating the field. Coach Willis and Coach Boots converse in the dugout as the second game of the double-header drags on. The field is pristine. The community has supported the success of the baseball program with top-of-the-line facilities and equipment. The lights and towers are the latest addition. They are state-of-the-art and the brightest available. The grass infield could be mistaken for a Major League Baseball team's grounds keeping.

The coaches' conversation turns to work. "How's the teachin' going?" Coach Willis queries.

"It's good to get to summer break," Boots responds with a shrug. "Don't get me wrong, I love teaching my geography class, but summers off and coaching baseball suits me better."

"You playin' ball this year?"

"Yup," Boots nods.

"You guys gonna be any good?"

Bootsy holds out his hand, palm down and twists it back and forth, "Eh, I think we'll compete."

The two coaches watch the action on the field a moment. "Three up, three down now, defense!" Coach Willis yells to his team. "Nothing but strikes out there, Gary!"

"I gotta ask you, Boots," Coach Willis turns his attention back to his assistant. "What the heck is it between you and Hillmann?"

Coach Booth dons a serious expression and shakes his head side to side, "He's just so damn cocky. It gets in the way of his ability. He's got so much potential."

Coach Willis' shoulders jerk with a small laugh. A smile curls his lips, revealing a Copenhagen grin, "A bit like you, I'm guessing."

"Not hardly!" Bootsy quickly retorts with a scowl. "I just don't want to see another 1987."

Coach Willis shakes his head as he looks out to the field, "For crying out loud, you gotta lighten up, Boots. That was two years ago. Let it go."

The men are silent for a moment as the action continues on the field. "That-a-baby, Gary! Way to throw strikes!" Coach Willis calls out with a clap of his hands.

The thinned out crowd from the bleachers reacts with a tired cheer. On the mound, Gary winds and throws a fastball for strike two, the Clarkston batter is frozen at the plate. Dave fires the ball back to Gary, "One more now, Buddy!"

The defense in the field behind Gary fires up the chatter, "He's a looker. He won't swing!"

Dave squats down behind the plate, "Let's put 'im away here, Buddy."

Gary stares toward home plate. Dave puts down two fingers for a curveball. With the slightest nod, Gary begins his windup and delivers a slow sweeping curve that starts behind the right-handed batter. The batter starts to jump out of the way, but freezes, his knee buckles in watching the ball break down and over the plate.

The umpire excitedly screams, "Stee-rike three!"

Gary jogs toward home plate, bearing toward the dugout to congratulate his pal, Dave, on a good pitch call. The rest of the team follows suit and heads to the dugout at the end of the inning.

In the dugout the coaches finish their conversation, "It was embarrassing losing the championship." Bootsy frowns.

Coach Willis spits his tobacco, "What are you talking about? We got second place! Just cuz we didn't win the championship..."

Coach Willis spits again, interrupting his own sentence and leaving a gap in the conversation that Bootsy jumps into. "I'm just saying," he pauses and shrugs his shoulders, "some people are starting to talk. They say you're slippin'".

Coach Willis waves away the comment, "Shit, right. Yeah, we win five, what six championships in a row...then we are runner-up and suddenly I can't coach."

Coach Willis spits in disgust. He digs out the chewing tobacco from his lip, stands and tosses the brown wad down to the floor of the dugout, and mashes it with his foot. Coach Boots stands and reads the batting order from the scorebook, "Aric up, Fitz on deck, Larry in the hole! Come on, now. Let's get some runs and ten-run rule 'em so we can get outta here!"

Coach Boots turns back to his head coach, who is glaring a death stare at him. "I'm just tellin' you what I heard," Boots timidly comments, punctuated with a shrug of his shoulders.

Coach Willis shakes his head. The dugout is a whirlwind of activity as the players enter from the field. "Those kids learned more from losing that one game than all the championships we won combined."

Boots hands the scorebook to Tony on the bench. He doesn't break eye contact with Coach Willis, "It's just what I've heard."

"Jus' drop it," Coach Willis says gruffly. "Take the third base coaching box. I'm staying in the dugout." He rubs his leg and looks to Tony, "Tony! Go coach first base! My leg is hurtin'."

Tony stands and balks, trying to figure out whom to give the scorebook to.

"Get going!" Coach Willis yells at Tony.

Tony flips the book on the bench and runs out of the dugout.

* * * * *

Fourteen year old Lawrence Thompson stands in the on-deck circle. He is Trent's younger brother and the right fielder. Lawrence waggles a bat in each hand loosening his shoulders. He sets the bats down as he watches the Clarkston pitcher throw a warm up pitch. Turning his attention to his batting gloves, he readjusts the Velcro straps and finally tucks in his large, fake gold chain hanging loose around his neck back into his undershirt.

He stands beside Aric Carson and Fitz, a.k.a. Patrick Fitzgerald, as they watch the pitcher toss a couple more warm up throws.

Lawrence smirks and drawls, "Yo, dogs. Git yo-selfs on, and I'll drive you in and put an end to this fiasco. You feel me?"

Fitz cocks his head as he looks at Lawrence, "Larry, ya realize you are not African American? You are White, right?"

Patrick Fitzgerald is fifteen years old. He is a personality vital to any team...glue to hold the unit together. He is the average Joe. He just gets things done with average looks, average strength, and average ability. His ruddy complexion and dark hair, with just a tinge of red along with his freckles, give away his Irish heritage.

Lawrence frowns, "Yo. Please lay off the 'Larry' stuff. Call me MC Lawrence or just Lawrence. That's the way I roll."

Aric rolls his eyes, "OK, Larry." He emphasizes "Larry." He shakes his head. "We'll set the table for you. You clean it up...Dog."

Aric Carson is the eldest son of one of the wealthiest farmers in the community. He has the best of everything: a new Chevy Camaro, custom baseball equipment, i.e., his own array of aluminum bats, spikes, helmets, and gloves. He is very generous with his possessions. He is big hearted, an appropriate match for this big, overdeveloped-for-his-age, boy.

Fitz snickers.

Lawrence holds up his fist, "Solid."

Lawrence holds up his hand and Aric slaps him five, but he grabs Aric's hand and pulls him to his chest for a quick hug. Aric panics, resisting, "What is happening?"

Lawrence does the same for Fitz. Aric and Fitz exchange pained looks after being caught off guard by the hugs. "What the hell was that?" Fitz questions.

Lawrence dips his chin, giving a nod to each boy. He points his chin to the plate, "Go up there and get a knock, brotha."

The new Clarkston pitcher struggles to throw strikes. Four pitches later, Aric takes first base with a walk. Fitz sits on the first toss suspecting the pitcher will not want to walk another batter. The ball floats in, and he laces a line drive just over the head of a leaping shortstop. With runners at first and second, the dugout and crowd perk up, wanting to end the game with a couple runs thereby enacting the long time mercy rule of being ahead by ten runs or more after five innings. A ten run lead has been deemed insurmountable at this level. Due to time constraints, the baseball powers have agreed that at such an occurrence, the game is over.

"Ducks on the pond, Law-dog!" Coach Willis yells from the bench, punctuating his encouragement with a spit of tobacco juice.

Ducks being the runners and the pond being the bases, the language of sports can be quite obtuse, but the phrase is echoed up and down the bench, "Ducks on the pond! Ducks on the pond!"

The "Law-dog" reference spouted by Coach Willis brought a few strange looks from the players. That was Coach Marvin Willis; the strangest things came out the man's mouth, and people were used to it.

"Now batting, the right fielder, Lawrence Thompson," crackles the public address system.

Lawrence steps near the plate and takes a couple of massive warm up swings. He drops the bat between his legs, re-tucks his gold chain, and adjusts his batting gloves, while staring down to the third base coach, Bootsy. Boots is going through a series of face touches, arm brushes, and taps to his hat, signaling Lawrence and the base runners what to do. "Come on, Lawrence. Swing away," Bootsy finally calls out with a clap of his hands.

Lawrence crosses himself and steps into the batter's box. The pitcher goes into his stretch, checks the runners, and grooves a fastball down the heart of the plate. The compact, inside-out swing of Lawrence launches a line drive to right-center field. Everybody is on the run with the clank of the bat. Coach Boots is a windmill at his third base coaching position. His right arm swivels round and round, waving in Aric followed closely by Fitz. Lawrence slides in just ahead of the throw to third base. The players break from the dugout and rush to Lawrence with pats on the backs and cheers of congratulations.

The public address system booms overhead, "That's the ball game, folks; ten to zero in the bottom of the fifth inning. Ten run rule."

The Clarkston team comes in from their defensive positions. The Reedville Teeners form a line and move towards the Clarkston dugout. The teams meet in a handshake line at home plate and tell each other, "Good game."

* * * * *

In the excitement of victory nobody even notices Coach Willis still on the bench. His hands are folded on this stomach, chin on his chest, and hat forward covering his eyes. He looks like he is sleeping with tobacco stained saliva dribbling from the corner of his mouth. It is Tony Osmond that notices the problem first, "C-C-Coach?" he stammers.

Tony is fifteen years old. Before the country's obsessive obesity fetish, Tony was just the fat kid with a stutter. Today he would be looking for a spot on the television show "The Biggest Loser: Kids Edition."

Tony reaches for Coach and gives his shoulder a shove. Coach slumps to the bench. "H-H-H-Help!" Tony screams. "Somebody, help! C-C-C-Coach is down!"

Gregory L. Heitmann

Chapter 6
Ambulatory

Tony's stuttering cries immediately attracted attention. Coach Booth summoned Reedville Police Chief, Rocky Miller. The chief had been in attendance for the Teeners' opener. He rushed to help the coach while chattering on his radio to summon emergency first responders.

Sixteen year old Annie Willis, Marvin Willis' favorite niece, rushed to her uncle's side from her post. Her duties for the evening had been scoreboard operator and public address announcer from the press box at the top of the bleachers. Annie had abandoned her position after seeing the commotion and flew down the stairs to help. She immediately suspected the problem. The crowd pressed forward around the dugout, curious to know what was going on. Annie picked her way through the mass of humanity to reach Marvin when she bumped into Gary as he gestured to the gathering gawkers, "Come on, people. Give Marv some room. The ambulance and EMTs got to get in here."

Annie pushes Gary away and kneels next to her uncle. "He's breathing."

She maneuvers her chestnut hair from her face and tucks it the best she can behind her ears. "I bet he didn't check his blood sugar; it's probably his diabetes."

Annie looks up and down the bench, "Where's Marv's duffle bag?"

"Over here with my stuff," Coach Booth grabs the bag and tosses it to Annie.

She tears open the bag and rummages through the gear finally pulling a case with a syringe and a vial. She loads the syringe and injects her uncle. Silence falls on the bystanders as Annie stands. "It's glucagons. His blood sugar was too low."

The ambulance and the emergency medical technicians arrive and take over the situation as Coach Willis starts to come around. In a moment they have an I.V. in his arm and begin administering fluids. With choreographed movements, Coach is on the gurney and being loaded into the ambulance. "Stop," Coach musters the strength to call out. "Where's Annie?"

Annie is instantly by his side and gripping his hand, "Right here, Uncle Marv."

Coach manages to smile, "Sorry about that, Annie. Can you get my stuff home?"

"Sure."

"Get my stuff, get my car, and then get your Auntie April to pick me up."

"Will do," Annie smiles.

Chapter 7
Mice to Neet You

Annie returns to the press box to finish her duties. She collects her scorebook and purse, finally shutting down the scoreboard. Moving outside, shutting the door, and fastening the clasp on the padlock for the door, she finds Gary Hillmann waiting for her. "Do you need any help?" he queries.

"I'm fine," Annie responds.

"Hi, I'm Gary Hillmann. I saw you down in the dugout earlier with the coach. You're Marv's niece?"

Annie smiles and extends her hand, "Hello, I'm Annie."

Gary grabs her hand and stammers a bit, "Mice to neet you."

Annie cocks her head trying to understand, "What?"

The look of horror on Gary's face passes in a flash as he shakes his head, "Umm, I mean, nice to meet you."

Gary lets go of her hand, "Listen, I can shut everything down and close up if you need to get out of here and see your uncle. I used to do the announcing and scorebook for the Legion and amateur games when I was a little kid."

"It's ok. I'm done. I gotta go."

Annie starts to move past Gary down the steps, and Gary follows. "Hey, if you'd like to get together and talk some time."

They continue to slowly navigate the bleacher stairs leading down from the press box. Annie twists her mouth, "I don't know."

"You know, it's weird. I didn't know Marv had any nieces...especially pretty ones. What's your story?"

Annie laughs, "You are blunt, aren't you? I'm just here for the summer staying with my Aunt April and Uncle Marv. I'm waitressing at April's Café."

"Wow, I go there all the time. Maybe we can just get together out there? You know...so we can talk?"

The pair reaches the bottom of the steps. Annie stops and looks Gary up and down, hesitating for a moment, "I gotta get going."

She pauses once more and sighs. She grabs a pen from the scorebook and grasps Gary's hand. Before he can react, she scrawls a number on his hand. "It's Uncle Marv's number. Just ask for me."

Annie turns and marches quickly to the parking lot with Gary watching her go. Finally he looks at his hand, "Wait…is this a five or a three?" He shakes his head as his voice trails off. "I guess she said it was Marv's phone; I can look it up," Gary says out loud, smiling and pleased with himself.

Chapter 8
Parking Lot

After the game, only two vehicles are left in the dimly lit parking lot; Dave and Gary are the last players to leave. Dave is just tossing his gear in the back seat of his Ford Fiesta. He slams the door and sees Gary approaching. Simultaneously they both ask the same question, "What are you still doing here?"

Dave grabs his wrist, "I was just icing my wrist. I took a couple balls off it tonight."

Gary shakes his head with a serious expression, "Two questions: Whose balls were they, and, as my best friend, why didn't you tell me that you were gay?"

"Shut up! Foul balls…foul tips. I'm the catcher! Foul balls!" Dave cries out in defense before laughing. "You know what I meant."

Gary laughs and tosses his bag into the box of his 1975 Ford F-150 pickup, "Sorry," he shrugs.

"And you? Where the hell did you disappear to, and why are you still here?" Dave asks accusingly.

Gary leans casually against this truck, picking at his fingernails. "Did you know that Marv had a niece?"

"Sure, Annie, that's her name, right? She works at April's Café, and I hear that she's going to be a lifeguard at the swimming pool this year."

"How did I not know this stuff?" Gary shrugs in surprise.

Dave opens his back door and begins to dig in his bag, "Where are my stupid keys?"

Gary presses his forearm against the window of the back door exposing the phone number on his forearm, "Need some help?"

Dave glances back, "Nah, I got it."

He stops digging, "Don't tell me…"

Gary smiles, "I gots her numba!"

"Wow, you don't waste any time, do ya?" Dave shakes his head and returns his attention to his search for his car keys.

Gary beams with pride, "You know it."

"Ah, here they are," Dave holds up his keys victoriously.

After a moment of celebration, Dave looks to the ground, "Dude, I've been meaning to ask you something."

Dave sighs and doesn't make eye contact.

Gary is intrigued by Dave's sudden change in demeanor and shrugs, puzzled by the stark contrast in behavior.

Dave stares down at his feet, "I overheard something...please tell me it ain't so."

He clears his throat without looking up, "I'm sorry, but I heard your mom say something to my mom about a packet in the mail from Kirtland. Isn't that the prep school out West?"

Dave finally looks up with pleading eyes, hoping for an answer more suited to his taste than what he anticipates.

Gary heaves an extended sigh, "Oh, God. I guess the word's out."

He meets Dave's eyes for a moment before looking into the distance. There is prolonged silence before Gary continues, "I've had some early contact with Pepperdine University; my uncle went there. Kirtland is a good prep school to help my chances for admission."

Dave's feelings are hurt, but he covers his wince well. He nods, "You're gonna leave me...to fend for myself? When were you gonna tell me?"

Gary shakes his head vigorously and holds up his hand, "Nothing's a done deal yet. Promise me you'll keep this under your hat for as long as you can."

"No problemo," Dave tries to smile, but can't. "But what about me?"

Gary shakes his head, "You'll be fine. Next year you will probably be working for your dad and his chain of restaurants. Where's the latest one, Bismarck?"

Dave sighs, "Shit, you're right."

Dave's posture has deteriorated to a point where he needs his car to hold him up, but now he stiffens, "Hey, good game tonight."

"Thanks, you too. Tough duty, catching both games."

"Tell me about it."

"Yeah, couple balls on your wrist..." Gary smiles.

"Stop."

Gary snickers, "You need the work. We need to get you in game shape. You are a great catcher, and, once we get you into condition, we'll get that hitting going."

Nodding concernedly, Dave agrees, "I definitely need to hit it harder."

Gary snorts, "That's what she said."

Gary heartily laughs at his own joke, "Thank you. Thank you. I'm here all week." He pulls at an imaginary necktie a la Rodney Dangerfield, while his comedy club audience of one shakes his head and smiles.

"I'm outta here," Gary waves as he reaches for the door of his truck and climbs in.

"Later, Dude."

Gary fires up his truck, puts it in gear, and tears out of the gravel parking lot, spraying a wave of gravel in his wake. Dave pops the clutch of his Fiesta while in reverse and spins a couple donuts on his departure. Gary rolls down his window and sticks his arm out. He extends a "big thumbs up" to his buddy on this driving exhibition as he proceeds down the block illuminated by the scant lighting of the streetlights.

Chapter 9
Practice...We're Talkin' 'bout Practice

Reedville Practice Field

    The daily grind of baseball is in full swing already. The day after the first games of the season, the boys are back on the field, taking batting practice against Coach Boots. Even with all the best game facilities that Reedville offered, the teams often settle for lesser practice amenities; such is the case this afternoon, sans Coach Marv. One of the keys to success of the Reedville baseball program is live pitching. Reedville coaching hit upon this theory early in the baseball program's development: the use of live pitchers for practice rather than a pitching machine. Seeing the ball come out of the hand of a pitcher is a crucial facet in training a hitter's mind and it just cannot be simulated by a mechanically thrown ball.
    This is a bare bones operation. There are no batting cages or netting set up to wrangle the balls. Batting practice is an open air event. The players stand around in the practice field and train themselves on the pop-ups and grounders off the bat of the hitter. Coach Marv wants to keep the players involved while hitters take their swings. What better training grounds are there than on the unkempt fields of the elementary school playground for learning how to field tricky grounders.
    The camaraderie is special during batting practice. Groups gather to shoot the breeze and joke around. The bonds of a team form here. From an outsider's perspective, they probably think it is a huge waste of time, this method of practice. One should never underestimate the sheer power of just spending time together, unified in effort.
    As usual, Tony holds court with his graphic stories built from his imagination, typical of a teenage boy, but completely unfiltered from his mind to mouth. The conversation is periodically interrupted as someone shags a fly ball or picks a grounder and simulates turning a double play

with the others in a "hot potato" fashion before tossing the ball towards the pitching mound, so it can be recycled into the hitting practice.

The locals recognize the practice, but a stranger passing by would be mystified by the seemingly unorganized activity. The dress is informal. No two players dress alike. The practice attire ranges from t-shirts paired with blue jeans to hoodies and shorts, along with a fair number of tank tops or "wife beaters" as they are affectionately known by the Teeners. The hodge-podge of clothes has all the undertones of an undisciplined, motley crew, but it could not be further from the truth. The old saying about being careful when judging a book by its cover could not be more applicable.

Tony gives a nod to Dave as a smile curls across his lips, "Gee, Dave, who was that woman that dropped you off at practice today?"

It's an on-going topic, and Dave shakes his head and frowns, but won't take the bait.

"I'm sure I'm not the first to say this," Tony continues. "But your mom is smokin' hot!"

"Shut up! You're a dick. You're talking about my mom!"

Tony's smile fades away, replaced with a serious stare as he looks Dave up and down. He shrugs, "Why are you so fat? Your mom has a kick-ass body." Tony waves his gloved hand at Dave, "But, then there's you."

The sound of an aluminum bat on ball clanks, and all eyes momentarily follow a line drive into right field where it is fielded nicely on a short hop by Lawrence. The small group recognizes Lawrence's effort, clapping on their gloves. Lawrence looks their direction and raises his glove in acknowledgement as the conversation turns back to Dave. "Tony, you would definitely know fat," Dave fires back.

"Hey! I'm big boned! If you know what I mean?" Tony grabs his crotch and pulls on it.

The bat clanks again, and Gary breaks from his position at Dave's side. He fields a ground ball and throws it to Fin Swenson. Fin is behind Coach Boots on the mound; he is shagging balls and making sure there is a steady supply in the five gallon bucket to be tossed to the hitter. Fin, fourteen years old, is one of the young players new to the team this year. He is ashen blonde, almost albino. He is tall for his age, a wiry-strong farm boy.

Gary rejoins the group that flanks Tony at a location somewhere between a deep shortstop position and left field. "Did anyone hear anything about Marv?" Dave asks.

"He's fine," Gary shrugs. "I heard it was his diabetes, like they said. I guess he was too excited about the first game of the year and forgot to test his blood sugar."

The bat clangs again, sending a deep drive to the outfield over the group's head. After that long ball they all tip their caps to Aric, now hitting and driving the ball deep.

"He's gonna be back, right?" Tony's voice wavers a bit, "Marv's coming back, isn't he?"

"He's gonna be out a couple days from what I hear," Gary responds.

Tony heaves a sigh of relief, "Thank, God! I don't think I could handle Boots as head coach. He's been just a complete dick lately."

Gary rolls his eyes, "Tell me about it."

The group follows another shot off Aric's bat over their heads. Watching the ball Gary continues, "He jumped all over my back last night when I missed that ground ball in the outfield."

Tony bursts out laughing, "Yeah, that was hilarious. You looked like a pee-wee player out there."

Tony imitates Gary's whiff of the ground ball, first waddling stiffly, then reaching for an imaginary grounder. Tony's face twists into a jaw-dropping expression of disbelief as he reaches into his glove for the imaginary ball only to realize it isn't there. He stumbles around searching for the ball before pretending to find it. Finally he mimes tossing it toward the plate. The group has a good laugh at Gary's expense, including Gary. "Come on, man. It wasn't that bad was it?"

Dave provides a comforting hand on Gary's shoulder, "Yeah, it was."

"C'mon. The grass in the outfield is practically knee-high!"

"Hillmann," Tony shakes his head. "Let it go; we forgive you; unfortunately, Coach Boots will never forget it."

The laughter resumes again.

Coach Boots looks back at the laughter with a scowl, "All right, break it up! Round 'em up! Dave, get in there and hit."

The players round up the baseballs into five-gallon buckets gathering at the mound. "Fin's gonna throw some batting practice," Coach Booth announces. "I'm gonna step behind the backstop and watch Dave swing the bat. Everybody stay alive out here. No goofin' off."

A murmur goes through the boys gathered around the coach. Boots points at Lawrence, "You're shaggin' for Fin."

Lawrence salutes as he pulls on his sagging shorts, "Aye, aye, Captain."

Dave steps up to the plate as Boots jogs around the backstop to observe. Fin winds and fires a strike down the middle with Dave taking a massive cut and miss.

"Easy, Dave," Coach Boots encourages softly. "Just make some solid contact."

Fin grooves ten strikes in a row, drawing "Hail Mary" swings and misses from Dave with nary any contact.

"Dave. You are going to have to cut down on your swing. Just listen to me," Coach Boots advises. "Come on, now. Square around and bunt a couple up the first baseline."

Fin winds and fires; Dave slides his hand up the bat and deadens the ball, sending it rolling down the first baseline. A cheer goes up from the players in the field.

Coach Boots smiles, "All right, we got contact. Couple more now."

Dave proceeds to bunt the ball perfectly. "Good job," Coach Boots nods and claps. "Swing away now!"

Fin rocks back and fires the first of six pitches, and Dave makes no contact.

Dave grimaces, embarrassed by his performance. He adjusts his batting gloves and helmet. Behind him, Coach Booth signals to Fin with both hands to ease up on the velocity. Fin acknowledges the coach with a nod, proceeding to lob the next pitch over the plate. Dave hacks wildly at the ball and makes contact enough for it to dribble twenty feet past the first base. Fin lobs four more to Dave with no successful contact.

"Couple more," Coach Boots calls out.

Two more pitches and two more whiffs end Dave's BP session.

"Don't worry about it, Dave," Coach Boots comforts. "We'll get you set up with a "T" and have you hitting off it into a screen to get the barrel square on contact. It's gonna take a bit, but I think I see what's going on. You ok?"

Dave nods, "Sure, Coach."

Dave takes his gloves off and stows his bat and helmet as the next hitter steps into the box to take some swings.

* * * * *

After every one got their swings in and practice was wrapping up, Coach Boots called the players together, "Get the equipment sacked up!"

The players stowed the bats and balls as Coach Boots looked at his note card. "All right, next practice...tomorrow...hitting same time. I also have a quick update on Coach Willis. He's fine and should be back after a couple days rest."

A car pulls to a stop on the street on the other side of the fence separating the elementary school playground turned practice field from the road. Lawrence cranes his neck, "Yo, is that Coach Willis?"

Everyone turns to look in the direction Lawrence is pointing. They see Coach Willis easing from his car as well as a young man emerging from the passenger side. Coach Willis limps by the silent huddled group and manages a wave as he makes his circuitous way along the fence with the young man to enter the practice field through the gate. The pair enters the playground and makes its way back to the group. Marv stands before the group and flashes a tobacco covered grin, "Hey fellas. They said I was supposed to take it easy, but I had to bring our newest player by. Meet your new teammate, Chuck Fisher!"

Chuck waves without a word and a few "Hi" and "Hello" grunts percolate out of the group. Chuck Fisher is a big kid for fifteen years old. He is six feet tall with a muscular 170 pounds rippling on his frame. His dark eyes, that some would say are "beady," hint at mischievousness. He looks at his teammates and makes eye contact with each boy as he nods and flashes his own happy-go-lucky smile.

"Chuck's mom, Lorraine," Coach Willis interrupts the awkward silence as he puts a hand on Chuck's shoulder and looks at his team. "Well, Lorraine asked me to introduce him as soon as possible. So, here we are; welcome aboard, Chuck!"

Coach Boots begins to clap, and the rest of the team joins the round of applause. The ovation dies away, and Boots nods toward Chuck, "Are you Lou Steven's boy?"

Chuck's voice cracks as he responds, "He's my step-dad. My mom just married him. We live on his farm by the river."

"Good, good," Coach Boots nods. "You helping out on the farm then?"

Chuck shrugs, "I try. I don't know much about farmin'."

"I gotcha," Coach Boots nods knowingly. "Well, what do you say? We just finished up with some hittin', but I can crank 'er up again if you want to take a few swings."

Chuck shrugs nonchalantly, "Sure."

*   *   *   *   *

"Let's go!" Coach Boots calls out.

The players scatter back to their accustomed fielding positions as Boots takes a bucket of balls out to the mound. Chuck grabs a helmet and bat. He steps to the plate and takes two stiff swings to warm up. Coach Boots holds up the ball, "Ready?"

With a nod of his head, Chuck signals he's ready. Boots lobs the first pitch in like a slow pitch softball, and Chuck cranks it to the asphalt between the practice field and the playground equipment adjacent to the elementary school. The ball takes two bounces on the asphalt and caroms off the brick school.

"Holy smokes!" Tony calls out in a high pitched whine of shock. "Did you see where that ball landed?"

Dave waves his glove at Tony, "Relax, that was a lob ball."

No sooner are the words out of Dave's mouth when he snaps his head around to see another bomb as Chuck rips the next pitch to nearly the same landing spot. Coach Boots throws faster and faster while Chuck keeps driving the balls deeply to every field. The players chase the balls off Chuck's bat and fire them back in quickly to keep the awesome display going. From behind the backstop Coach Marv looks on with a country-mile-wide smile, "Looks like we got ourselves a *'Natural'* here."

Chapter 10
Pegasus

April's Café is informally known as "Pegasus" because the Mobil Oil Company sign with the winged-horse still stood erect outside the diner years after the leaking underground fuel tanks had been removed. Pegasus is a place for teens to come, hang out, and slide quarters into arcade games. Just south of the main intersecting highways in Reedville, Pegasus provides ample parking for teens and coffee-drinking farmers to do the same thing, hang out and gossip. The evening crowd of patrons competes against the Dairy Queen for those who are on hiatus from home cooking, but this afternoon was fairly quiet. Most of the men coffee drinkers were in the grasp of the season's chores, spraying or providing chemicals to spray the crops. Two shriveled farm hands, long since retired, sit at the far table with coffee. On the other side of the building, the arcade side, several members of the Teener team mark time before the late afternoon practice.

Tony racks the balls on the pool table. It is Tony and Fitz pitted against Gary and Dave. Tony carefully lifts the plastic triangle from the formation of billiard balls. Nodding to Gary, who is ready to blast the cue ball for the break, Tony shrugs, "Why don't we make it interesting, say for five bucks?"

Tony turns his back to hang the rack on the wall as Gary fires the cue ball across the green felt of the table with an ear-splitting crack.

"Keep your money, Tone," Dave laments.

The eight ball breaks from its protected center position within the racked-triangle and slowly rolls toward the corner pocket. Fitz, leaning heavily on his cue stick, butt sticking out, slides and wriggles trying to transfer body English to the eight ball to keep it from the pocket. Tony turns around in time to see the black ball drop out of sight. He stands slack-jawed and motionless.

"Wow!" Dave exclaims beaming a big smile, "I don't think I've ever seen that before!"

Gary smiles and shrugs, placing his cue stick on the table, "Well, like my grandpa always said, 'Better to be lucky than good'."

Dave holds a hand up and Gary slaps a high five, "Dude, check out the twins."

Tony and Fitz stand like statues, stunned by the sudden beginning and end of the game. "You know," Gary points at them, "you two slack-jawed yokels could pass for brothers, if not twins, with expressions like that."

Dave laughs the words, "Yeah, Fitz's new nickname: Tony-Twin."

Fitz snaps out of it, sputtering and stammering, "Oh yeah? It's you Dave; you're the Tony-Twin, all big-boned. We should get you two matching scooters, and you could go around as the *Guinness Book of World Records* fattest twins."

Dave blanches, hurt by the words, but his friend piles on. "He's kinda right," Gary winces and holds out his arms, rounding over his belly, "you guys are...big."

Dave shakes his head in disgust. "How dare you?" he asks with a British accent. He smiles unable to refrain from laughing at his own expense. Gary clamps down a firm hand on Dave's shoulder, "Don't worry, Dave. It's just baby fat. When you reach puberty, it will probably melt away."

"Shut up!" Dave whines.

The group of boys enjoy the laugh, but after a moment the giggling of young girls overtakes their joke. Lawrence plays a pinball machine in the corner of the room, slapping the buttons to activate the pinball flippers. The machine chimes and whirs as the ball bounces off the bumpers. Fitz, Tony, Gary, and Dave exchange chagrined looks as the young girls fawn over Lawrence. "Yo, Lawrence!" Gary calls out. "Can you come here?"

Lawrence holds up a finger momentarily and without turning around yells, "Give me a minute!"

The young girls surrounding Lawrence stare daggers in Gary's direction. Sending the indignant message, "How dare he interrupt their man?"

Dave is puzzled by Gary calling over to Lawrence, "What do you want Lawrence for?"

"Well, boys," Gary explains, "it's probably for the best that we had a short game. I am headin' over to the swimming pool to talk to Annie."

"What?" Dave's voice hits a high note. "What makes you think she'll even talk to you?"

Gary smiles, "Hey, she's a captive audience. She's stuck lifeguarding. She's not going anywhere."

"Ooh, that's a good plan," Dave nods in agreement, joined by Fitz and Tony with their concurring head nods.

"Yo, Lawrence!" Gary calls again.

Lawrence turns and quickly acknowledges Gary with a nod before turning back to his game. Lawrence's attire is attention grabbing. His baggy, over-sized jeans mysteriously defy gravity. He sports a white, wife-beater tank top. Fake gold chains drape around his neck. Dark Elvis Presley sunglasses cover his eyes; finally his ensemble is topped with a red bandana, folded and tightly tied, covering his head. Lawrence grabs the closest girl's hips and slides her in front of himself, putting her at the controls of the pinball machine. He nuzzles her neck, and the teeny-bopper shivers. Lawrence yells across the room, "'Sup, G?"

Lawrence gently touches the other two girls' shoulders and whispers, "Ladies, take over my game," before he sidles away from the pinball machine.

He moves across the room, strutting as if a jungle beat courses through his head. Fitz and Tony laugh and shake their heads, watching the spectacle. "Yo, G!" Lawrence extends his hand; Gary clasps it, and they pull in and bump chests. "What can I do for my homeboy?"

"MC Lawrence," Gary drawls, "I need you to do me a solid, soul brotha."

"What you talkin' 'bout?" Lawrence recoils. "Anything for you, G."

Gary gestures to Dave, "I need you take my place as Dave's partner and play some pool against these clowns." Gary points a thumb to Tony and Fitz.

Reaching into his pocket, Gary extracts four quarters and slaps them on the pool table. Lawrence sneers at Tony and Fitz, gawking over at him. "I'm down with that," Lawrence mumbles extending his fist.

Gary bumps his fist on Lawrence's. Tony grabs the rack and re-racks the balls on the table sans the eight ball, "The nine is the new eight," Tony declares. "We'll salvage this game."

"Where you off to?" Lawrence calls to Gary who is heading for the door.

"Gonna lay down my rap on Annie," Gary grins.

"All right," Lawrence nods approvingly.

Gary gives a thumbs up and a nod to Dave as he pushes open the door and exits.

Lawrence turns to his competitors as he picks up the cue from the table, "Which of you suckas is gonna break?"

Tony meekly raises a hand. Lawrence flicks the cue at Tony. "Drop each other's cocks, and let's play some pool."

Dave moves to his partner and puts his arm around his shoulder, "Come on, MC. This is just a friendly game of pool. We're not gonna hustle 'em."

Lawrence manages to replace his competitive scowl with a smile.

"That's the spirit," Dave encourages. "Now, pull your pants up. I'm tired of looking at your underwear."

Chapter 11
Road Trip

The Reedville Teener Team shares transportation for road games with the other baseball squads of the town. The not-so-glamorous transport is a school bus rented for summertime use from the Reedville School District. The big yellow bus with the words "SCHOOL" covered by duct tape (for legal reasons) accomplishes the basic needs of moving the boys from game to game. Thirty to forty mile trips on a bus is no problem for the young, resilient "men" bouncing along the highway to Bridgewood and this day's doubleheader. The team passes time in a number of different ways. For the moment, the music is down, and the players are hushed. Leaning forward toward the aisle from their seats, the boys look on as Gary and Tony stare stoically at each other in silence. Moments pass, and the boys are jostled by the stiff suspension of the bus traveling over Highway 137's rough pavement, but they are oblivious. A raspy whisper cuts through the silence, "Come on, Tone," as Aric encourages his buddy.

Tony and Gary continue to stare at each other expressionless. Whispers spring up among the players, swelling up and down with the noise of the tires on the road. Players fidget in their seats. They sport different states of their uniforms. Some are in shorts and t-shirts. Some wear three-quarter sleeve undershirts with their uniform tops already donned, ready to put their pants on and play.

Tony's jaw moves up and down, but no words come forward. His bottom lip quivers and his head starts to shake side to side.

"I'm calling it," Dave breaks the silence raising his hands. "Gary is victorious in this round of the sick-off."

Tony's quivering lip is not a sign that he is about to cry; no, he blinks rapidly as he stammers, "D-D-D-D-D-Damn it!"

Tony slaps down his hands on his bare legs, sporting only shorts, "I-I-I-I thought I had y-y-y-you today!"

Half the players cheer and half groan as Gary is recognized as the winner. Everyone relaxes a bit, taking a collective breath after the competition. Gary imitates Tony, exaggerating every blink, twitch, and stutter, "Th-th-th-that's the b-b-best y-y-ya can d-d-d-d-do?"

Tony waves a chubby hand at Gary, "E-e-e-enough, Gary. You're the best."

Gary smiles and shakes his head, "You know what they say about imitation being the sincerest form of flattery?"

Tony nods affirmatively.

"Well, in your case, Tony, it's not flattery I provide; it's mockery."

Tony shakes his head, bewildered, "I-I-I don't know where you come up with this s-s-s-stuff." His faces twitches and ticks as he speaks.

"You are good competition; I'm just lucky you have a sister who's slutty. It's like an eternal spring of sick commentary I can draw from."

Gary looks around the bus, "Quick show of hands. Who has had their hands down the pants of Tony's sister, Jan?"

About a third of the boy's hands go up in the air. Tony and Gary survey the results.

Dave looks at Tony, "Shouldn't your hand be up, Tony? I think we've all heard the stories."

The bus roils with laughter. "J-J-J-Jesus, Dave! Who asked you?" Tony fires back.

Gary laughs, "It's ok, Tone. You know what they say about incest."

Dave finishes the thought, "Incest is best!"

Dave punctuates the statement with a finger held high in the air, and he receives a high five from Gary. Tony spits and sputters as he clenches a fist. "Take it easy, Tone. We know it's not true with you, but that can't be said about all the other guys with your sister."

Tony's eyes fall to the floor. He finally finds a bit of shame, "Wh-wh-what can I say? My sister likes boys."

"Speaking of liking boys," Gary looks at Tony. "I just read in the paper that one in twenty-five people is gay according to a new study's statistics." Gary eyes the players on the bus, "We got over twenty five guys on the team; statistics would say we have one gay guy here." Gary smiles, "Is it you, Tone?"

Boisterous laughter echoes over the road noise throughout the bus. "It's n-n-n-n-not me!" Tony roars.

Gary shrugs, "Statistics tell us different. If not you, then who?"

Tony turns his gaze to the front of the bus. Fin sits effeminately posed, cross-legged, eating a banana, and flipping through a magazine not paying attention to any of the going's-on.

The eyes of everyone else follow Tony's stare. "Touché," Gary calls out. "But, I think we all consider Fin to be 'sensitive.' He's not like you, who we all think of as 'flaming.'"

"Sh-Sh-Sh-Sh-Shut up! I-I-I-I concede you win!" Tony whines. "Mercy already. How can I top your line about J-J-J-Jan's snail trail? I-i-i-it's just unfair!"

Dave jumps into the commentary, "Come on now, we've all seen Jan in her bikini at the swimming pool. Everyone has seen the luscious lips and can imagine the snail trail."

Dave high fives Gary.

"Lay off, D-D-D-D-Dave," Tony whines some more. "That's my s-s-s-s-sister."

"Huh," Gary grunts. "I thought you might jump on Dave's mom, but I hear everyone does that."

Tony reaches and slaps Gary a high five. Dave rolls his eyes. "Et tu, Gary? Get off my mom."

Gary looks concernedly at Dave, "It seems we hear that too often, Dave."

Laughter rolls up and down the aisle.

"What did I do to draw your wrath?" Dave questions Gary.

"I'm sorry, man. I'll stop."

Tony is not to be denied. "Face it, Dave. Your mom's a h-h-h-hotty. She's like a l-l-l-lightning rod."

Tony stands and swivels his hips. "I'd like to strike her with my lightning."

Everyone has a good laugh observing Tony's gyrations as he clasps his hands behind his head and looks skyward, hips twitching wildly.

"Wait a minute," Gary interrupts. "I don't get your metaphor. Dave's mom has a rod?"

Howls of laughter rip through the bus as Gary continues, "Her rod," Gary puts his index finger into a circle formed by his thumb and finger. "This is you," Gary says holding up the circle. "This is Dave's mom's rod," Gary holds up his index finger.

Gary puts his finger in the circle, "Am I getting this right? You and her...Is she wearing some sort of strap-on dildo?"

More howls of laughter bombard the bus at Tony's expense. Boys are wiping tears from their eyes. Tony stands at the center of attention, his vibrating hips have stopped. He smiles and waves his hand in front of his face, bowing as if before royalty or a karate master toward Gary, "My sensei."

Tony sits and players settle back in their seats and begin getting uniforms on as they approach Bridgewood. Tony digs through his duffle bag. He puts on his jersey and while doing so, a tube of eye black falls to the floor and rolls across the aisle to Gary's neighboring seat. Eye black is the anti-reflection concoction an athlete puts under his eyes, across his cheeks, in order to cut down on the glare from the sun or the harsh lighting of the towering field lights. It comes in the form of a triple-sized lip balm tube, more like the size of a glue-stick.

"Hey," Tony calls to Gary. "Th-Th-Th-Th-Throw me the eye-cock. There, by your f-f-f-f-foot."

"What are you talking about?" Gary responds without opening his eyes as he relaxes.

"The eye-cock, the t-t-t-t-tube of eye black n-n-n-n-next to your foot. Y-y-y-you know, the anti-glare stuff?"

"I don't know what the hell you are talking about. Eye-cock?" Gary remains with his eyes closed and blindly reaches down near his foot, finally grasping the tube. He brings it to his face and opens his eyes, examining the container.

"Any n-n-n-noun in the English language can be substituted with the w-w-w-w-word cock. It's easy. In this case it's even better. Eye b-b-b-black already has a 'C-K' at the end, so it makes even m-m-m-more sense."

Gary shakes his head and sarcastically replies, "Yeah, it makes total sense."

He tosses the tube back to Tony. Tony twists the cap off the tube, exposing a shiny black, over-sized lip balm applicator-looking thing. He draws a line on each cheek.

"Th-th-there. Check it out," Tony smiles displaying his decorated face.

He holds up the tube, "If you notice, the t-t-t-tube itself is c-c-c-cock shaped, h-h-h-hence, eye cock.

Tony stands and holds the eye black tube at crotch level as he twists the end of the tube exposing an ever increasing amount of eye-black, "L-l-l-l-look at my big, black c-c-c-c-cock, everybody!" Tony hollers. "Anybody else n-n-n-n-need some eye-cock?"

Gary laughs, "I'll wait until closer to game time before my eye-cock, thanks."

Tony acknowledges Gary still holding the tube at his crotch, "Just l-l-l-l-let me know," he continues in a Brooklyn accent. "I got your eye-cock rightchere."

Tony yells louder across the bus, "Eye-cock! Anybody else n-n-n-n-need some eye-cock!"

At the front of the bus, Coach Boots drives, leaning sleepily over the steering wheel. He is oblivious to any of the antics going on behind him. In the seat immediately behind the driver, Coach Willis sits. He is already clad in his uniform, but without an important finishing touch...his leg. His artificial leg is detached in his lap. He ties the cleated-shoe at the bottom of the prosthesis. He rubs the stump of leg that remains to try to ease some of the tingling that never seemed to go away following the amputation.

At the back of the bus, players get themselves dressed for the game as the stereo plays the song "Love and Affection" on the radio. "Love and Affection is by the rock duo Nelson. Probably much less than the majority of the people know the rockers. Nelson are the twin sons of Ricky Nelson, with their long, golden locks, and one hit. You might recognize them if you saw their rock video. "C-C-C-C-C-Crank it, Lawrence!" Tony cries out.

Lawrence blasts the boom box volume, and, when the chorus arrives, the team sings along with a modification to the lyrics "I can't live without your love and affection." Instead they sing, "I can't live without your cock and erection!"

Gregory L. Heitmann

Chapter 12
Company

The bus ride home from Bridgewood is quiet and dark. The team played well and won the first game handily with untouchable pitching and timely hitting. The second game dragged on until all hours. The Reedville second string was getting experience. Neither team was able to throw strikes, and a walk-fest had ensued. The teams combined for 23 base on balls, and the five inning game ended at 25 to 15 in favor of the Bridgewood Teeners. Coach Willis and Coach Boots were able to glean valuable information in the game regarding reserve players and their ability to step up if needed.

The bus finally pulls into the Pegasus parking lot at ten minutes to midnight. The squeaking brakes and jerking halt of the bus initiates groans of awakening players as shuffling of gear punctuates the end of the trip. As raucous as the day's road trip had started, it is ending as docile as a house cat. One by one the players file out of the bus. No words spoken, the only communication is a nod or grunt as they move down the steps and across the gravel parking lot to their cars lined up at the far end of the lot. Several of the younger players have a parent waiting for them, and engines fire to life and headlights flicker on as these players find their rides home. Dave and Gary finally exit the bus and stroll with no urgency toward their vehicles. "Looks like you got comp'ny," Dave whispers a warning to Gary.

"What the…," Gary reacts to the dash lights of his truck providing a backlit glow to a silhouette positioned in the passenger seat.

Gary approaches his truck carefully. The windows are down, and he can hear music from the radio drifting from the truck. He finally recognizes the figure perched on the seat of his truck and relaxes. "Annie?" he states questioningly.

Dave shrugs at the statement and arrives at his car. "Later, man," he calls out as he gets in his car with minimal departing words.

Gary gives a silent wave to Dave as the Ford Fiesta cranks and cranks before firing up. With a clunk of the transmission, the car is in reverse and whines as it backs up. Dave shifts it into first gear, releases the clutch, and throws gravel at Gary. Gary smiles and waves again at Dave already out of the lot. Moving forward to his truck, Gary tosses his gear into the back. He opens the driver's side door and climbs in.

"Hi," Annie coos softly as she reaches to turn the volume down on the radio.

"I see you found the key," Gary nods.

"Your ultra-secret key hiding spot, under the floor mat of all places, was no match for my brilliant mind." Annie adjusts the radio volume up a notch again. "I hope you don't mind."

"No. It's ok. Why are you here so late?"

"Uncle Marv is coaching, so somebody has to shut things down at the café. We were cleaning late, so I just stayed and waited. How did the games come out?"

"We split. Our second string needs some work, but I think we're pretty good."

A long silence blankets the cab of the truck as Annie stares at Gary. "I enjoyed our conversation at the pool," she says looking away.

"Me too," Gary nods.

His head bobs to the music from the radio while he fine tunes the volume knob. Annie's eyes search Gary's expression. "Listen," Gary finally interrupts the silence. "It's late. Do you need a ride home?"

"Yeah, but let's not go quite yet. I was kinda hoping to continue our conversation. Maybe we can...talk."

Annie leans over and kisses a surprised Gary. He gathers himself and returns the gesture. Putting a hand on her shoulder, she pulls away a bit, breaking the kiss. "I'm listening," Gary whispers, sliding Annie toward him across the bench seat.

Chapter 13
With a Bang

It is day in, day out for the summer baseball leagues of Reedville. There is no off-day for the kids. Maybe, just maybe, there might be a long weekend associated with the Fourth of July holiday or a Sunday without a game, but for the most part, it was baseball all summer long; live, breathe, eat, and sleep baseball. You have to love baseball or you are not going to make it through the three month gauntlet of hardball. The Teeners that are on the team are there because they love it. They have come through the "minor league system" of the community, the Pee Wee League and the Midget League. Everyone is familiar with the expectations, and they meet the criteria. No one quits. The ones that can't hack it are weeded out in the Pee Wee or Midget levels. Some just never go out in the first place.

So the grind continues. Batting practice the day after the late game is sluggish, but it commences and wears into early afternoon. Coach Willis and Coach Booth lean on the batting cage behind the hitters, observing and critiquing each hitter's swings against Fin. Fin is throwing batting practice, but more importantly, he is unknowingly trying out for a pitcher's spot in the rotation. "What do you think of Fin?" Coach Booth thrusts his chin in the general direction of the pitcher's mound as he rests his weight against the batting cage.

Coach Willis is in a similarly relaxed pose taking in the practice. Both coaches are dressed in blue jeans and western shirts; sleeves rolled up mid-forearm. They could be mistaken for a couple cowboys looking through a screen, observing cattle coming to the auction floor of a sale barn, but here they are evaluating the talent that could be run out on the green field of a baseball diamond, not a pasture. Coach Willis drops his head and spits down between his feet, "Fin's good 'n' wiry. Most of all he can throw strikes."

Coach Willis spits again and focuses on the steady barrage of straight strikes grooved by Fin to the batter. "We got to get 'im to change speeds and get a curve ball going. He'll get racked if he's only got that one pitch."

"Yeah," Coach Booth nods in agreement.

"No, that was a good call, Bobby," Coach Willis complements his assistant. "You thought Fin could throw, and man, it looks like you picked a winner."

"Thanks, Coach," Coach Booth manages to smile.

The steady clank of metal bat on ball rings out in rhythm. The coaches continue to watch a few more strokes before Coach Willis bellows, "Next hitter!"

There is a pause as balls are gathered, and the new batter steps in.

Fin rocks and fires strikes to the plate, and the hits resume to clang off the bat of the hitter. "Where's J.W. at?" Coach Willis questions.

Boots points between first and second base, "He's over near second base."

"I want J.W. to get some playing time."

"What?" Coach Boots questions. "Why? He is terrible."

"I want to see if he can play at all. We need some people in reserve if we get dinged up a little."

Coach Boots shakes his head discouragingly, "I'm pretty sure J.W. is not cut out for this game."

The coaches watch as a blooping pop-up flares out above J.W.'s head. He staggers and stumbles underneath the fly ball. He awkwardly settles under the ball with his glove ready. The ball slaps into the pocket of his glove and bounces out harmlessly to the ground. Joseph Wesleyan Keats is a rookie to the team this year, a consummate nerd with dark-rimmed athletic glasses, including a strap. His slight buck teeth currently under the taming powers of orthodontic braces give him a slightly mentally diminished appearance. He is average size for his age and doesn't seem un-athletic if standing still. Put him in motion, and he is a danger to himself.

A scoff and near borderline guffaw emanates from Coach Booth as he waves a hand at J.W. "Look at that kid out there." Coach Booth shakes his head with exaggeration, "This level of competition has surpassed his ability."

"He tries hard," Coach Willis notes, scratching his chin and squinting to the outfield. "What the fuck is Tony doing out there?"

Tony has one of the new younger players in a bear hug and is dry-humping him as four or five other players observe.

Coach Willis elbows Coach Booth, "Tell 'im to knock it off."

Coach Booth cups his hands around his mouth and yells, "Tony!" Coach Booth says nothing else; he just shrugs his shoulders and sticks his hands out in question while shaking his head.

Coach Booth's yell has caught Tony's attention. His humping slows and stops as he releases the rookie. He picks up his glove, and his arms flail as he continues to tell a story to his crew of regulars gathered in their usual spot. Both coaches observe Tony flapping his arms and gyrating oddly. His mouth moves a mile a minute, and the coaches can't hear the conversation, but soon Tony is humping the air, wildly thrusting his hips. The boys around him laugh and double over. A batting practice grounder zips to the side of Tony, and he flicks his glove at the ball, stopping it. He gestures to everyone watching, trying to make sure everyone saw his feat. He jumps up and down and re-enacts throwing the glove over and over again.

Coach Willis squints out at Tony, "Jesus! What is wrong with that boy?"

The other kids point at Tony and then back to the glove. They shake their heads, and Tony beams with pride, finally ambling over to pick the glove up with the ball in it.

Coach Booth sighs, "I don't even know where to begin."

Both coaches watch from a distance and see Tony twitch and stutter, embellishing his story as his gums flap non-stop.

After a minute or two of silence between the coaches, the conversation continues, "Well, Boots," Coach Willis spits tobacco between his shoes. "What do you think of the rest of the team?"

Without hesitation Boots answers, "Best team in the north part of the state…by miles…near as I can tell."

"I would agree," Coach Willis' mouth forms an unconscious sneer of agreement as he nods.

Coach Boots stares out as Fin keeps throwing strikes for batting practice. He flips a thumb in the mound's general direction, "Even with Fin, we could still use some more pitching."

"Could always use more pitchin'." Coach Willis spits and wipes his mouth. He continues to spit small efforts, trying to remove a few stray grains of tobacco from his lip. "I don't wanna rush Fin. How about the new kid…Chuck?"

"I suppose."

The men turn their attention out toward Chuck, shagging fly balls in the outfield. The clank of the metal bat is immediately echoed by a sickening, deep thud of horsehide on flesh. Fin has taken a line drive off the side of his head. The distinct thump of a ball to the head is the same hollow thump of testing a ripe watermelon with a rap. Fin's follow through on his pitch puts all his weight on one leg. From such a delicately balanced position, that stanchion crumples on impact. Fin falls face first, his momentum rolling him forward onto his back. He laid there flat on his back unconscious, limbs spread eagle.

"Holy shit!" Boots cries out lurching forward and clawing his way around the batting cage attempting to get to the field.

He finally sprints out to Fin and kneels down at his fallen player's side. Removing Fin's glove, he lifts Fin's head and gently rests the boy's head on the leather. The players slowly gather around, inching forward in shock. Stunned silence grips the team. Fin moans, surprising the players, and they take a step back in fear, but after a moment return to their encircling ways. Fin's eyes blink open, and he regains consciousness. He stares up at his teammates eclipsing the sky. His mouth moves without sound before he finally is able to speak, "Hey, everybody."

Coach Boots lets a shallow gulp of air out and breathes deeply, not even realizing he'd been holding his breath, "Oh, good. I thought maybe you were dead."

Coach Willis finally ambles forward, pushing away the boys as he makes his way through the circle of players. "He awake?"

Boots gives the coach a nod and half-hearted smile.

Fin blinks crazily as he stares skyward barely seeing the faces staring down at him, "What happened?" he questions. "Hey, everybody," he repeats.

Fin starts to sit up but groans and wobbles a bit before Coach Boots pushes him back down, resting his head on the glove. "Uhh, just stay down, Buddy," Coach Boots comforts the player.

A goose egg size welt is protruding from Fin's head, causing his white hair to stick out. Fin touches the bump and winces. There is a trickle of blood reddening his shock of pale hair.

"It's 'mazing his head didn't split wide open," Coach Willis notes.

Boots turns his attention to Fin, "You took a liner off the side of your head."

"Hmmm," Fin contemplates. "I don't remember that. What was I doing?"

Coach Boots looks up at Coach Willis with a bit of panic in his eyes before looking at Fin and speaking in a long, drawn out statement turned question, "Ummm, throwing batting practice?"

"Nope, doesn't ring a bell," Fin's head lolls side to side on the glove as he denies the incident.

Coach Boots looks up wide-eyed at Coach Willis, "Boots, get 'im home. Talk to his folks and tell them to be sure he gets a doctor's appointment. I don't want to see him back at practice 'til he's got a note from the Doc."

Boots pulls Fin to his feet. Fin's rubbery legs barely support him, and the coach practically carries the boy off the field. "Dave," Boots calls out, "go bring my car around. The keys are in it."

Dave takes off jogging toward the parking lot as the Coach eases Fin slowly out of the facility. The team watches Fin's tentative steps, mesmerized, before finally being brought back to baseball. "Chuck, get up there and throw some," Coach Willis claps his hands and shouts. "Who's up? Somebody get in the cage!"

Batting practice resumes, barely missing a beat.

Gregory L. Heitmann

Chapter 14
Wheaties

The full day of baseball continued into the evening for Bobby Jim Booth. He is back at the baseball field after delivering Fin to his mother and making sure Fin received medical attention. Fin's mother, Gloria, had a meltdown seeing her baby injured and in pain. Bobby offered to take both of them to the emergency room, and he stayed with mother and child three hours until Fin was released. The diagnosis was a concussion; the remedy was a week off and a return trip to the doctor if the headache lasted more than three days.

Bobby has returned for his moonlighting job, playing catcher for the Reedville amateur baseball team. He is probably in the best shape of his life, and his play reflects it. When Bobby steps to the plate in the bottom of the first inning, those aren't "boos" coming from his own dugout. His teammates howls in unison, "Boooooth."

The resulting cheer sounds more like a pack of howling neighborhood dogs, annoying players and fans alike. The more agitated people got, the louder and longer the "booing" continues.

The "boos" are momentarily silenced and replaced by cheers on the first pitch Bobby sees. He likes the pitcher's fist pitch fastball and drives the ball deep into the darkness. "All right," Bobby acknowledges his work and flips the bat after admiring it, maybe a little longer than he should.

He circles the bases in a brisk jog, finally touching home plate. The umpire watches the spikes hit the center of the home plate and through his mask addresses Bobby going by, "Geez, Bootsy, you are on fire."

Bobby shakes hands with his teammate coming to the plate, pauses momentarily, and turns. Flexing his bicep for an instant he smiles back at the ump, "I've been eating my Wheaties."

Boots continues walking to the dugout. As he descends the steps every player is there to provide congratulatory high fives, helmet slaps, and handshakes.

Chapter 15
Hot Dog

    The games pile up, and experience comes with it. Another home night game for the Teeners under the lights exposes the tedium associated with the long games and long season. Chuck, the new kid, was now a fixture in centerfield. He is positioned next to Gary in left field. There is no issue with fielding assignments; Chuck's extraordinary speed is the perfect match for the position. He covers seventy-five percent of the outfield, leaving the right fielder and left fielder to split the remaining twenty-five percent. Gary is quite content with the defensive split. He feels he is more cut out to the offensive side of the game and handing the defensive reins to Chuck is peachy keen as far as he is concerned. The team is still looking for a starting right fielder, so there is a steady rotation of young players through that position. The youngsters very much appreciate Chuck's assistance out in the field.

    Tonight's game against New Rockford shines a light on the chink in the armor of the Reedville Teeners. Chuck did not come up through the ranks of the Reedville baseball system. The Reedville Cardinals system teaches the fundamentals. Making the routine play is the key to success and continues to be a philosophical pillar for the baseball community. Learning the fundamentals and committing them to second nature as a player is just the way it is.

    "I got it!" Chuck hollers as he jogged under a high pop fly.

    He waves his arms reinforcing the fact that he does indeed have it. Gary throttles back his run to back up the play as Chuck camps under the fly ball; Chuck positions his glove near his waist in preparation for a basket catch. Trent playing at shortstop is ambling toward centerfield pointing to the ball and getting into position to be the cutoff man. The cutoff man is another fundamental part of the game. He is the player that moves toward the outfield to provide a relay for the ball when the ball is hit to the deeper part of the park. Instead of trying to heave the ball all the way from a long distance in a high loop, cutoff men are dispatched to relay the ball back to the infield with shorter, quicker throws. You can evaluate a team fairly quickly by how they handle the simplest relay from the outfield. Does the cutoff man get depth? Does he get his hands up as a target for the outfielder to quickly acquire where to throw the ball? Is he properly aligned by the infielder or catcher where the play might challenge a base runner? These are all basics learned at the lower levels of baseball. However, first and foremost, is using both hands to make the catch. A simple, necessary foundation of defense...catch the ball with two hands.

"I got it!" Chuck calls out once more.

But he doesn't have it. The ball bounces off the tip of Chuck's glove scampering away like a frightened chipmunk. Gary kicks it back into high gear and stabs the miscue, quickly firing the ball toward the infield, hitting the cutoff man, Trent. By the time Trent turns to fire the ball home, two runs score on Chuck's error.

Gary expressed his displeasure without holding back. Both dugouts and members of the crowd heard Gary's side of the conversation, "What the hell are you doing?"

Chuck shrugs, "I'm sorry, man. My bad."

"Sorry? Catch the fucking ball with two hands...above your head; like you were taught!"

Chuck shakes his head, "You're right. You're right." He holds up his hands, "I'm sorry. I'm sorry. It won't happen again."

Gary turns back toward his position in left field. He takes a couple of walking steps and shouts over his shoulder, "I don't want to hear it. Just do it. You just do it as you were taught."

The loud discussion is not unnoticed by the Reedville coaches in the dugout. "You want 'im out?" Boots questions Coach Willis.

There is no immediate answer.

Boots queries again, "You wanna sit Chuck down?"

"Turner!" Coach Boots yells to the end of the bench.

Coach Willis looks at Boots and shakes his head from side to side.

Turner acknowledges his name, "Yeah, Coach?"

"Never mind," Coach Boots stands, folds his arms, and paces the dugout.

The inning ends with a ground out third to first, and the team runs to the dugout; everyone except Chuck. Chuck walks to the dugout and is the last to climb down the steps. Everyone notices Chuck. Gary shouts from the opposite end of the dugout, "Show some hustle!"

Chuck is incredulous. He grabs the front of his jersey as if to say, "Are you talking to me?"

That pushes Gary's button. He stomps down the dugout, spikes crunching on the concrete floor littered with sunflower seeds. Gary stops short of Chuck who is already defending himself, "What did I do?"

Gary's hands are out from his side as he gets in Chuck's face. "Where do I start? Your hot-dogging cost us two runs. Then you have the nerve to lollygag all over the field, embarrassing all of us as you take your sweet time coming back to the dugout."

Chuck swallows hard as Gary's lecturing continues, "The only person that has permission to walk off the field at the end of the inning is the pitcher. He's working his butt off out there, so he's earned it. I expect you and everyone else to sprint off the field after the third out. If you don't see me sprinting off the field, it is your duty as a member of this team to remind me to run. It should be a race to the dugout after the third out…period."

At the end of the dugout, Coach Boots starts to stand ready to intervene, but Coach Willis grabs his elbow and pulls him back to the bench. "You want to handle this?" Coach Boots asks.

"No, no," Coach Willis whispers. "Let's let it play out. They got to be able to police themselves."

The coaches look on with everyone else. Gary is in Chuck's face, but Chuck is not backing down. There is silence in the dugout before Dave finally stands and approaches, putting a hand on Gary's shoulder and pulling on him slightly. Gary shrugs Dave's grasp away without breaking the stare down with Chuck. Gary finally speaks slowly and clearly, "If you don't want to be part of this team, then just get out of this dugout right now."

Chuck nods almost imperceptibly and looks away for a moment. He focuses back on Gary, "You're right. I'll do better."

Gary's voice is calm, and he speaks with a tone that is low and slow, "I don't want to hear your lip service. Just do it."

Chuck and Gary stare at each other beyond the comfort level of the dugout. Again, Dave puts his hand on Gary's shoulder. Chuck gives the slightest of nods and sits on the bench stowing his hat and glove. He starts to adjust his stirrups and stockings.

Gary turns and heads to the far end of the dugout. The team does not look at either player. The dugout is tense and silent. Gary stomps down the dugout, clapping his hands, "Let's get some runs!"

He sits on the bench and dons his batting gloves, claps again, and calls out, "Let's go! Who's up? Who's on deck?"

Chapter 16
Caper

Boys will be boys. That old corollary has no trouble proving itself, especially in a small town. Summertime in Reedville provides two activities: baseball and the swimming pool. If you were a son of a farmer, you had a third activity, chores. For energetic teenagers with limited options, boredom sets in fast. Without school in session, idle hands become the devil's workshop.

Chuck has come into town from the farm early for practice to hang out with his new friends and teammates. Jesse Ford and Turner Jackson are joining Chuck in the freshman class at Reedville High School this fall, but for the time being they enjoy a midday cruise of the Reedville streets. Chuck drives his farm truck up and down Main Street, observing the steady stream of grocery shoppers in and out of the Supervalu.

Jesse Ford bore an ironic name, being the son of the head automotive technician at the Chevy dealership. He is small for his age. Sunken eyes along with his rail thin frame give the appearance that Jesse is malnourished. Turner is also small. His parents both work as teachers in the Reedville School District. Turner's dark complexion and black hair are traced from his father's Armenian lineage. Jesse and Turner are best friends, and now they invite Chuck into their posse. Chuck is nearly a foot taller than his new friends, but that difference doesn't bother them; it is a distinction that bonds the boys.

Within a half hour of cruising the streets, they have a plan. Chuck parks the truck, and the boys head to the drug store. When the door opens, a bell rings, indicating a customer is in the store. The clerk looks up from her position at the register and exchanges smiles with the trio as the boys march to the candy aisle. They stalk up and down the aisle, eyeing the shelves alone in the empty store. "Ok, you guys ready," Chuck whispers. "You guys go up and talk real loud as you grab a couple Cokes. I'll lift us some candy bars."

Turner is getting cold feet, "I don't know, man. My mom will be pissed if I get in trouble."

Chuck picks up a candy bar and sets it back down, "How can you get in trouble for talking? I'll be doing the stealing. Now get up there."

Jesse pushes Turner toward the front of the store, "Come on, Turner. Let's go."

Jesse and Turner raise a ruckus as they reach into the cooler near the register and grab sodas. They laugh and joke when they hear Chuck yell to them, "Hey, grab me a Coke."

Jesse waves a hand acknowledging the order, and the boys move to the register. Chuck eyes the clerk from the candy aisle. When she turns her attention to the sale, he begins grabbing candy bars left and right shoving them into his pants.

"Three Cokes. That'll be a dollar and three cents," The clerk sings out the phrase.

Jesse hands over the money, and the pair begins to move out of the store as Chuck approaches the register, "I'll be out in a minute. I gotta pay for this candy bar. See you at the truck."

Back at the truck Jesse and Turner wait, sipping on their Cokes. After a moment Chuck opens the driver's door and shielded by the truck, he opens the button on his pants and a dozen candy bars spill out on the seat.

"No way!" Turner cries out.

"That was genius," Jesse shakes his head. "Distraction, and then you further divert attention by actually paying for one? That was awesome."

Chuck pushes the candy bars across the bench seat of his truck and climbs behind the wheel as he buttons his jeans. He fires up the truck, and the trio drives down the street eating their spoils. They turn off Main Street and in front of them the water tower stands high above the trees a half mile away at the end of town. Chuck raises a finger from the steering wheel and points to the tower, craning his neck a bit to get a full view of the sentry standing watch over the town. "You guys up for a real adventure tonight?"

Turner and Jesse look at each other and shrug. "Sure, I guess," Jesse mumbles through chewing on a candy bar.

Chuck takes his hand from the steering wheel and points to the water tower dramatically, "Tonight is a rite of passage for young men. We are going to leave our mark on the water tower."

"Whoooaaa!" Turner gasps.

"Man, I don't know if that's a good idea," Jesse chimes in still struggling to chew his caramel candy bar.

"C'mon. You guys scared?" Chuck prods his buddies as he drives slowly down the street approaching the tower.

Without hesitation Jesse shouts, "Yeah! I'm scared."

"How high is that thing?" Turner cranes his neck to get a better view of the tower as they get closer and closer.

"You been up to Rock Lake Refuge?" Chuck asks.

His passengers nod. "That observation tower is pretty much the same height as this water tower."

"Huh," Jesse grunts. "This tower seems higher."

"It's gonna be awesome!" Chuck exclaims with enthusiasm. "We're going to turn the 'Home of the Reedville Cardinals' into the 'Home of the Bluebirds'."

Chuck points to the bed of the truck, and the boys turn to see a tarp covering something in the back. "Check it out. I already got some blue and orange paint. We'll do it real subtle. We'll just repaint the bird. I bet nobody even notices for a couple days!"

After the late day practice and an evening swim at the pool, the trio of budding Michelangelos proceeds to work on their masterpiece under the cover of darkness. With the help of bolt cutters to pinch the lock off the tower ladder, they scale the landmark and go to work. As promised, the work is subtle, very professional; it is a project that would make Mrs. Carter, the junior high art teacher, proud.

Chapter 17
Bluebird

The afternoon doubleheader finds the Reedville Teeners competing against Brayton. Reedville could be considered a suburb of Brayton, about half the adults that live in Reedville commute the twenty miles one way to their jobs in Brayton. Brayton has a population of about 25,000 and is home to the Mid-Dakota State University Fightin' Pronghorn. The baseball game today is at Pronghorn Field, part of the MDSU campus. The field is a little nicer than Reedville's, but the dugouts are a considerable upgrade. They are part of the athletic complex for the university and attach to locker room facilities. The Brayton Teeners are in the highest division of state baseball leagues for Teener teams in South Dakota. The population of the city is ten times that of Reedville with that many more athletes to choose from, but that doesn't thwart Reedville. Brayton Teeners are being thumped fifteen to zero in the opening double header game. The Reedville dugout is relaxed while watching Chuck mow down Brayton batters. "How's the amateur league treating you?" Coach Willis question Boots.

"It's all right," Coach Boots shrugs.

"Modest. I hear you're yanking homeruns out left and right."

A clank of the bat turns the coaches' attention to the game, an easy ground ball rolls to Trent at shortstop. He flicks the ball to Jesse covering second base, who relays the ball to Tony at first base, turning a perfect double play to end the inning.

"Hey! Way to go, boys!" Coach Boots yells out as he stands and claps, moving to the opening of the dugout and climbing the steps. He greets the players hustling off the field with high fives.

Lawrence pops up from the bench to join Boots in welcoming the team back to the dugout. He passes by Coach Willis, "Hey, Whigger, you hit for Hillmann and go to left field," the head coach drawls.

Lawrence stops and points to himself, "Are you talkin' to me?"

Coach Willis is taken aback, "Yeah, I'm lookin' right at ya. Who'd ya think I was talkin' to? Get up there, Whigger!"

Coach Boots retreats back to the dugout, looking around nervously, "Uh, Coach, you might want to lay off that nickname."

Coach Willis is mystified, "What ya talking about? That's what I hear everyone calling Lawrence. What's the big deal?"

Coach Boots leans in and whispers to Coach Willis. Coach Willis' eyes widen from their near permanent squint, and he nods. "...so, that's why we refer to him as Lawrence when we are out in public," Boots continues as he pulls away and finishes his explanation to the Coach.

Coach Willis turns to Lawrence, standing frozen looking at the coaches, "Gotcha," Coach Willis signals to his assistant and flashes a thumbs up. He turns to Lawrence, "You deaf, Lawrence? Get up there and hit?"

Lawrence bounds up the dugout steps, grabs a helmet along with his bat, and warms up with a few practice swings.

Reedville slaps Brayton around twenty to two in the first game and scores seventeen in the second game of the doubleheader to win seventeen to seven in a shortened game.

The equipment is being sacked after the game, and Coach Willis watches the players stash the equipment in the army issue duffle bags. "The team seems to be playing pretty good, eh?"

Coach Boots nods, "Things seem to be roundin' out nicely."

Coach Willis yells, "Load up! Let's get on home!"

In less than a half hour the team is pulling into the parking lot of April's Café. A police cruiser sits in the parking lot, and, when the bus turns into the lot, the door opens and the chief of police steps from his car. Chuck is the first to notice the policeman. "What are the cops doing here?" he asks pressing against the window for a better look.

Gary looks up from his relaxed position stretched out across his seat. He sits up and joins Chuck looking out the window. They observe Chief Miller rotating his "Smokey Bear" type hat nervously in his hands as he waits for the bus to stop and Marv to climb down. "I don't know if you know this, but Marv is the Mayor of Reedville. He's the Chief's boss. Something must have happened," Gary answers Chuck's question.

The team has all moved to the one side of the bus to see Marv and the Chief talk. A couple players start to gather their stuff and move to the front of the bus to exit. "They're pointing to something," Chuck notes as he looks out, trying to follow the direction of where the Chief is pointing.

The team can see Marv shrug, and the Chief points with both hands toward the water tower.

"I'm getting' off the bus," Gary states, gets up, grabs his gear, and moves down the aisle.

Chuck follows Gary, and they move down the steps of the bus and out into the beautiful summer day. Passing by the Chief and Marv, the boys can hear the conversation. "So, our beautiful red cardinal looks like a bluebird. Somebody painted it!"

"I can't see it from here," Marv squints into the blue sky with just a few wispy clouds floating high above.

"Let me get you the binoculars," the Chief moves to the car, grabs a pair of binoculars, and hands them to Marv.

Marv looks through the optics and cries, "My bird! My beautiful red bird is blue!"

Marv hands the glasses back to the Chief, "Let me guess; you have no suspects."

The Chief shakes his head side to side, "Shoot, I'm not even sure when it happened. I just got a call from somebody asking if I had noticed the water tower. Son of a gun, I went out to look at it and saw it just this morning." The Chief scratches his head, cocking his eye toward the tower, "Funny thing is...they did a pretty good job."

Chuck and Gary stand a distance away and listen to the conversation. "Dang it, Chief! You figure out who did this! I loved that big red bird!"

Coach Willis is still in his uniform. He spits tobacco between the Chief's feet. "I'm on it, Marv...I, er, I mean Mr. Mayor," The Chief puts his hat on and salutes as he backs toward his cruiser.

Gary calls out, "Why don't you call around and see if the hardware stores in town or Brayton sold some blue or orange paint?"

Chuck's face turns ashen, and his mouth drops open. Marv points at Gary, "You heard him, Chief. Get on the horn and see if the stores sold any paint."

The Chief salutes again, "Aye, aye, Sir." The head policeman gets in his cruiser and spins out of the gravel lot.

Gary waves to his teammates, "See you later, guys." He heads to his truck and all the other players do likewise, except Chuck. Chuck stares at the water tower. He wonders how long it might take for the Chief to make the connection with the paint he bought. He hopes the Chief is as inept as he seems, if not inept at least too lazy to look into the matter.

Gregory L. Heitmann

Chapter 18
Rock Lake

A Reedville Teeners trip to Rock Lake is typically an unusually joyous event. The short fences at the small town baseball park are attractive targets for the Reedville hitters. Rock Lake did not field much of a team from year to year, and this year is no exception. The final score may have been twenty four to nothing in favor of Reedville in just three innings, but that didn't mean the Reedville Cardinals left unscathed.

It started during the fielding practice session. The usual routine was shortened, Coach Boots hit a couple fly balls to each outfielder, the fielders threw the ball to the cutoff man, and the ball was relayed to the appropriate base when called out by the coach. Next, the outfielders are summoned to the dugout, and Coach Boots hits grounders to the infielders. Rock Lake Baseball Park is not what would be considered modern. In fact, opposite of state-of-the-art is the best description. The first grounder to Trent at shortstop ricochets off a stray stone and takes a wicked hop to his chin. The skin split, and Trent was done for the day, taken to the emergency room and treated with a butterfly bandage to help minimize scarring.

After the fielding practice debacle, the team is called into the dugout. Once in awhile Coach Willis likes to harken back to the old days and provide a pep talk, a few words of inspiration to the team. This is the game the old coach chooses to motivate his team. Coach Willis paces before the team as Coach Boots reads the starting lineup. Once the lineup is set, Coach Boots gives a nod to Coach Willis, "Men, listen up. It's not everyday we have a chance to do extraordinary things." The coach clasps his hands behind his back and limps back and forth across the dugout, eyeing each of his players. "I want each of you to go out there and play hard!" His voice rasps and rises, emphasizing the final word.

A few smiles begin to appear on the faces of his young audience. Coach Willis continues, "We play some stiff competition out here, and I know each of you will rise to the occasion."

A few stifled snickers ripple through the boys on the dugout bench, and more smiles are attempted to be hidden with a strategic hand in front of the mouth. Coach Willis turns his back and looks far off into the distance across the field. His speech continues now, softer, "We started small, but we've gotten bigger."

Giggles are not contained as more and more of the players are unable to stifle the mirth. Coach Willis wheels and faces his players with a serious expression, "We don't want to come up short...use your heads and don't pull any boners out there!"

It's nearly painful for players to keep from all-out laughter. Boys are covering their mouths and their shoulders twitch and heave. Coach Willis points a finger at the boys and waves it back and forth in front of the team, "Let's go out there and stick it to 'em!" He continues, pecking his finger at each player as he limps by each boy, "Play hard! Play hard! Play hard!" the coach calls out for each of the players as he passes them in the dug out.

"What's all this sniggerin'?" Coach Willis looks to Coach Boots for answers, but Boots is no help as he holds a hand to his mouth cursing his own laughter. The riotous amusement can no longer be contained. The entire dugout is busting a gut in laughter. "Get your hands in here," Coach Willis sticks his hand out, and the rest of the players, still in the throes of laughter, put their hands one on top of each other. Coach Willis calls out, "On three, Cardinals...One, two, three,"

With one voice the players shout, "Cardinals!"

They fall back to their seats on the bench trying to recover from the speech. Dave sits next to Gary and elbows him, "Rousing speech, eh?"

"A-rousing," Gary quips, "I think you mean a-rousing."

The two laugh as they get their batting gloves on and get ready to lead off the game in the top of the first inning as the visiting team.

Three players had multiple home runs in the game including Gary, Chuck, and Aric. Even Dave showed some signs of life in his bat with a homerun before taking a foul tip off his protective cup and exiting the game early. Lawrence filled in as catcher for the rest of the game and continued to impress the coaches with his versatile set of skills. Another casualty of the rough field was Tony at first base. He took a wicked shot off his groin in the second inning, "deflecting the ground ball with two balls of his own," as the dugout politely put it. He had gone "cupless" for the game and paid the price.

The game is in the books, the players exchange handshakes, and the equipment is sacked and ready for loading. Coach Boots carries the bat bag to the bus door before pausing and waiting to get on. He realizes he has left his jacket in the dugout. "Aric, put this on the bus," Boots says, leaning the army duffle bag against the side of the bus before turning and jogging to the dugout to retrieve his coat.

The exact events are not clear, and consensus after the fact places the blame on the coincidental events capped off by the field lights shutting down as Boots returns to the bus. How is he to know that Aric never heard him say, "Put the bag on the bus?"

In any event, Boots hustles back to the bus and leaps up the stairs and into the driver's seat, never seeing the bag leaning against the bus in the dim light. He fires up the engine, puts the bus in gear, and starts to pull away. The bag slides off the side of the bus, and, when the back tire rolls over the bag, it causes quite a lurch. "What was that?" Boots cries out as he grinds the bus to a halt.

He kills the engine, swings the door open, and bounds from the bus. Fearing the worst, that he has run over a person, he quickly breathes a sigh of relief upon discovering it isn't a body under the bus, only the bat bag. Players stream off the bus in the dim illumination of a street light and witness something that would have been humorous if not so tragic. Boots unlatches the duffle bag and begins extracting bats from the bag. One by one, he pulls out bats that sport the curvature of bananas. Players look on in shocked silence. All the bats are worthlessly bent beyond use. "Aric!" Coach Boots shouts. "I told you to get the bag on the bus! Look at these bats!"

Aric cowers back as Coach Boots approaches him, "I-I-I-I never heard you!"

"H-H-H-Holy Shit!" Tony yells as he picks up one of the curved bats and holds it to his groin, "Maybe I can use this as a cock replacement. I'm going to need a new dick after that wicked grounder today."

The team looks on in laughter as Tony's shadow casts an interesting image against the side of the bus as he waggles his artificial member.

"You know what?" Aric decrees. "My dad will buy us some new bats. Don't worry about it!"

It is that bizarre trip to Rock Lake that stamps its brand on this one-of-a-kind season for the Reedville Teeners.

Chapter 19
Tony's Theory of Relativity

    The Reedville baseball system uses the same warm up methodology at every level of baseball from Pee Wees to Amateurs. The first thing you do when you get to practice is find your partner, get a baseball, and play catch. This warms up your arm and body to get them ready for activity. The improvement in the eye-hand coordination that you get from the routine practice of catching a baseball and throwing a baseball cannot be over estimated. An ordinary person can see the massive improvement a Pee Wee player can make in just a week's time once instructed in the art and science of throwing a baseball. This simple warm up exercise hones motor skills at every level of baseball. Go to any Major League baseball park, and you will see the professionals playing a simple game of catch.
    This group of Teener players is somewhat unique in that playing catch to warm up, also is therapy. It is an open discussion on anything that comes to mind, and it is most notoriously lead by Tony. No subject is private or sacred. The conversations in the therapeutic outfield grass are confidential, as far as anyone knows. This is the same for pretty much anything said and done on the diamond.
    It is a different world now at the Teener baseball level compared to the previous stages. This is the first time the players form an all male squad, whereas, in the lower regimes of baseball, the Pee Wees and Midgets, there were always a few female players interspersed through the teams. The smattering of female players had previously tempered the crude conversation that seems to occur without diversity in groups. Conversations degrade to the gutter for the Reedville Teeners; their talk often starts at that point and stays there.
    For today's workout, before batting practice, the warm up commences, and Gary tosses the ball back and forth with Dave. The lines of players form on either side of Gary and Dave. Each player tosses the ball back and forth with his partner. It is a relaxing exercise to throw the ball back and forth, a way to ease into the competition of the practice. It is no surprise that Tony's opening salvo for today's conversation starts

bluntly. "You kn-kn-kn-know what I don't get?" Tony ponders loudly to his neighbors warming up in his vicinity.

Nobody takes the bait, and it is a rhetorical question from Tony, which he in turn answers with his own brand of oration. "I d-d-d-don't understand a skinny k-k-k-k-kid like Fin or Trent," Tony pauses, baseball in hand. He extends a finger in the direction of his specified teammates. "H-H-H-H-How in the world do those guys have huge horse cocks? Meanwhile m-m-m-m-m-me and Dave here, us big g-g-g-guys have these stubby, little dicks."

"Hey!" Dave calls out from his position next to Tony. "Speak for yourself!"

"Wh-wh-wh-what?" Tony rolls his eyes. "I've s-s-s-s-seen you in the shower after gym class. Y-Y-Y-Y-You got nothing to brag about, D-D-D-Dave."

Dave shakes his head incredulously. "Why you lookin' at my junk?"

Tony shrugs. The players continue to play catch. Today's topic brings a lot of uncomfortable laughter to those within earshot of Tony's observations, but it doesn't generate much conversation. Tony picks up the slack in the commentary. "I-I-I-I have a theory though," he continues. "H-H-H-H-Hear me out now," Tony tosses the ball to his partner, Aric, as the conversation continues. "I-i-i-it's all about relativity. I-i-i-it just looks like my d-d-d-dick is small because my body is so b-b-b-big."

Tony is very satisfied with his theory. A long silence falls across the boys warming up their arms. It's Fin who finally breaks the silence, "First of all, Tone, thanks for noticing. I'm sure you'll get the word out for me and Trent." Fin throws the ball to Trent, who tosses it back. Fin holds the ball a moment before pointing to the moon in the sky. It's not a full moon, probably only three quarters full. "I think Tony is onto something with his relativity theory. I saw a PBS show on TV, and it talked about the moon." Fin tosses the ball to Trent, "The show analyzed the optical illusion of the moon and how we see it in the sky."

Fin points to the moon again with his glove as he catches the ball from Trent. "It's the same moon we see on the horizon. But, if you notice when the moon is close to the horizon, especially when it starts to get dark, it looks huge!"

Fin nods in Tony's direction, "It's all relative."

Tony smiles, satisfied in Fin's support of his theory. "Wh-Wh-Wh-What do you think? You th-th-th-think we should have a c-c-c-c-cock measuring contest then?"

"Enough about your cock already, Tony," Dave pleads.

"That's n-n-n-n-not what your mom said," Tony retorts. "W-w-w-wait a minute," Tony points to the parking lot. "That's y-y-y-y-your mom right now in the parking lot."

"Oh, God," Dave sighs as he spies his mother getting out of his car and getting in her own vehicle.

Most of the team has stopped playing catch and are peering toward the parking lot a hundred yards away. Dave shakes his head. "Her car was blocking me in on the drive way, so I took her car and told her to come and switch cars if she needed her own back."

Tony waves and hollers, "Hi, Mrs. Brown."

In the parking lot Mrs. Brown waves back. She disappears into her car and drives away. "Oh, m-m-m-my goodness," Tony moans. He reaches down the front of his pants. "Oh, my…m-m-m-my cup is getting too tight."

"Shut up! That's my mom! You dick!" Dave yells.

Dave winds up and tosses a baseball underhand with some velocity at Tony's crotch. The ball meeting the back of Tony's hand down the front of his pants, emits a loud crack. Tony howls in pain and warm ups are over.

Chapter 20
Summer Time

Annie and Gary spend as much time together as they can manage between Gary's baseball schedule and Annie's multiple work requirements. It is a summer romance, everything is as fresh and new as it can be for a teenage courtship. They both understand how fragile the relationship is in combination with the fall deadline when Annie would leave Reedville and return to her parents in Minneapolis. They are careful not to waste time arguing, rather they just pursue enjoyment in each other's company.

It is a hot summer, and Gary visits the swimming pool often. He is "rescued" multiple times by Annie. It is always the same; Annie jump downs from her lifeguard chair and pulls an "incapacitated" Gary floating face down from the water. Mouth to mouth resuscitation is applied with amazing results.

Unfortunately, ten year old boys are observant. They liberally ply their own versions of needing rescue, and a couple dozen boys are banned from the pool for a week along with Gary.

The Monroe County Fair marks the midpoint of summer. Annie and Gary have the best time riding the Ferris wheel. From the top of the ride, as they look across the fairgrounds below and beyond, they can see the flat prairie farmland spreading in every direction. The Ferris wheel is the highest point in the county when the fair is in town, and it provides a unique perspective for its riders. Annie and Gary come back to the ride at night to see the lights from above. It does not disappoint, and it is here that the young couple exchanges their first "I love you's."

If the county fair marks the halfway point of summer, the Fourth of July holiday puts an exclamation point on the passage of the season. Annie's parents visit and meet Gary at her family's lake cabin on Pickerel Lake up in the hills, a short hour-long drive from Reedville to the Glacial Lakes Region. This Fourth of July holiday is unusually cool. This suits Gary and Annie just fine. They are able to sit close under a blanket holding each other tightly while enjoying the fireworks reflecting on the lake.

They are both naïve: blissfully ignorant enough to enjoy each other's company without dwelling on the finality of summer break. Soon the holiday hiatus is over, and Gary is back with baseball and Annie back to waitressing and lifeguarding jobs.

Chapter 21
The Rumor

After the Fourth of July holiday, the homestretch of the baseball season begins. The final third of the season is left for the Teener team. This is the time of tune-up games, a conference tournament, and then the run for the state title. Tonight, for the twilight double header, the Teeners are lined up across from each other playing catch to warm up in the outfield. Gary is flanked by Dave on one side and Tony on the other. They toss the ball back and forth to their partners about 100 feet away. The tosses get slower and find more of a pause between each throw as the warm up winds down. Lawrence approaches the group, "Did you hear the rumor?"

Gary tosses the ball to his partner and quickly retorts, "Tony's pregnant? Yeah, I hear that all the time. But he's just fat."

"No, man," Lawrence's face scrunches in a serious fashion. He looks in toward the dugout. "My dad said he heard a rumor that Boots signed a thirty-day minor league contract. He's heading out this week."

The three boys look at Lawrence as if he has a third eye in the middle of his forehead. "What are you talking about?" Gary questions incredulously.

"I'm serious," Lawrence raises his right hand. "I swear it."

"Why in the hell is he still here then?" Dave shrugs.

"That has to be just a rumor," Tony states knowingly.

Fin moves closer to the group, having overheard the conversation. "I saw in the paper the other day that Boots had hit something like twenty home runs in fifteen games this last month in amateurs."

"Holy crap!" Tony cries out. "Maybe it is true. Gary, go ask him."

"Forget it! He'll jump all over me about minding my own business. You know how he is."

The group stares into the dugout. Their warm ups have stopped, and now they just look questioningly toward their coach sitting in the dugout making out the lineup for the game and chatting with Coach Willis. Coach

Boots looks up from the scorebook to the outfield and sees the players just standing around. He waves the players in to get the game going.

With the lineup set, Fin is left in the dugout and assigned to pry into Bootsy's rumor. Fin keeps the score book and sits close to Coach Booth. His mind churns as he ponders how and when to ask the question about the minor league contract. Reedville is out in the field, and fewer personnel mill about in the dugout to distract and taunt him. Fin is ready to begin his inquisition of the coach. He is in thought staring blankly down at the scorebook. He is not paying attention to the game as he sits in Reedville's home dugout along the third baseline. The dugout has a protective screen, but the steps to enter and exit the dugout are open. The opponent's left-handed batter takes a weak swing and fouls a baseball on a looping line toward the dugout opening. "Look out!" Coach Boots yells as he leaps out of the way.

It is too late for Fin. By the time he snaps to the present, the ball has caromed off the back wall and catches him flush on his right cheek. The scorebook flies through the air, and Fin slumps to the dirty dugout floor. Coach Boots shakes his head as he kneels down to pick up Fin. "Lawrence, go get some ice from the concession stand."

Lawrence runs from the dugout, and Coach Boots props Fin on the bench. Fin's eye is swollen shut already, but he is conscious, holding his hand gingerly over his eye. "Can you see?" Boots asks.

Fin groggily answers, "Yeah. I'm all right."

Lawrence is back with a bag of ice. The concession stand keeps a healthy supply of ice bags for just such incidents, whether it is a foul ball in the crowd or dugout.

Fin holds the ice on his eye and leans down and scrapes up the scorebook. "Why didn't one of you guys stick out your hand and protect me?" Fin hands the score book to Lawrence, "Here, you keep the stupid scorebook."

"No problemo," Lawrence smiles. "You guys gotta protect me from foul balls though." Lawrence waves a warning finger to everyone in the dugout. "Swear y'all will protect me."

The ruckus in the dugout preempts any questions directed toward Coach Boots, and the night goes on without answers for the rumors. Reedville trounces the weak Appleton team in both games of the double-header. Spirits are high in the dugout after the game ends, and the handshakes are completed at home plate. Coach Willis releases the team from bagging up the equipment as a reward for their play. That is the congratulatory speech he makes in the dugout when he volunteers Boots and himself to stow the equipment for the night, but the head coach has an ulterior motive. He wants to speak to Boots about the rumor. "I saw your name in the paper again...two more home runs. Wow."

"Yeah," Boots responds as he shoves catcher's equipment into the duffle bag Coach Willis holds open. "I wanted to talk to you about that."

"What? You need some hittin' tips? I don't think I can help you there."

Boots laughs as the men toil putting bats, balls, and helmets away. Coach Willis can't find the words to ask his assistant about possibly leaving the team and the moment passes. Mentor and protégé are left to do the dirty work after a good night's effort on the baseball field.

Chapter 22
Call Up

Bobby Jim Booth walks into his empty, darkened house after 10:30 pm. Kicking off his spikes, he pads through the small two bedroom, one bath, single story bungalow in his socks. He closes the blinds and notices the flashing light of his answering machine before even turning on a lamp. The only illumination of the house is the microwave oven's digital light and a faint glow of the street light penetrating the lowered blind. Bobby moves to the phone and picks it up, listening for the dial tone; he hesitates and hangs the phone back up. He presses the answering machine button, and a robotic voice cuts through the air, "You have…two…new messages."

The machine beeps, and a man's voice, polished in the art of doing business over the phone sounds out, "Hey, Bobby. This is Rodney Nelson with the River Dogs. I was hoping to catch you to discuss the 30-day contract we tendered. Give me a call back and let me know if you have any questions. We could use you down here. Thanks."

Bobby unbuttons his jersey and heaves a heavy sigh. It had been a long day. His head hurts from contemplating the contract offer he had received in the mail that morning. It had arrived in a large, official, padded, 12" x 15" envelope with the River Dogs logo stamped in place of the return address. Bobby had received a call from Rodney Nelson three days ago with a verbal offer. He could barely breathe when he heard the proposal to play professional baseball. He managed to give Rodney his mailing address and was able to avoid hyperventilating. Three days later it was scary. It should be simple, having a dream come true; getting paid to do something you love…playing baseball. Who would imagine they would pay you to play. Play! The word they use is play. You don't "work" baseball, you play. Bobby's head pounds and he rubs his temples. The answering machine continued, "Hi, Bobby," a woman's voice softly cooed. "I was hoping we could talk. Call me."

It was Jeanie. Bobby and Jeanie hadn't spoken in a couple weeks. Their strained relationship was put on an extended hiatus after a momentous argument about Bobby's time away either playing or coaching baseball. Jeanie had thought she could handle it, but Bobby's mistress was baseball and it was dominating his life. Jeanie was jealous, and Bobby made his choice...it was baseball first in his life for now.

Jeanie's voice took Bobby aback. He managed a smile, still in the dark. He reached for the phone again, but put it down. He was not ready to talk to Jeanie, and a discussion about a minor league contract would probably only throw fuel on the fire. Finally flicking on the kitchen light, Bobby pulls out a chair from the table and collapses unto the stiff, upright, wooden piece of furniture. He digs through the pile of papers on the table and finds the River Dogs envelope.

The answering machine light stops flashings and it beeps signifying the end of the messages. Bobby turns his attention to the envelope. He stares blankly at the envelope and the logo of the River Dogs on the return address, tracing his finger over the embossed stamp. Finally, he extracts the contents and flips through the contract for the tenth time that day. Who ever imagined that trying to follow a dream might be so gut wrenching?

Chapter 23
Sunflower Daze

The warning shot that summer is nearly over, and fall is approaching for Reedville, is the Sunflower Days Festival. If it were still the 1920s, people would probably refer to the festival as the "cat's meow." Luckily it is the 1980s, and everyone has electricity and indoor plumbing. Sunflower Days is a long weekend starting on Friday night with live music until the wee hours of the morning then recommencing with more entertainment early Saturday afternoon and into the night. The barricades are up and the sun is down. Charlie Boyd and the Ropers, a popular local country band, are kicking it, the second act of the night. The street dance is a popular South Dakota summer activity. It seems there is an endless rotation of festivals or celebrations every weekend for each small town in northeast South Dakota. Tonight is Reedville's night. The town's population has swollen to triple its size as people of all ages wander around Main Street. Protected by ropes, saw horses, and wooden barricades, traffic is barred from the Central Business District this weekend. Laughter rings out from every corner and the din of conversation competes with music from the stage. The beer garden is a stagnant mass of men and women trying to quench a thirst.

A block away from the stage Gary and Annie stand in the crowd swaying to the music. Annie smiles, swings her hips, and raises her hands over her head while enjoying the music. She shouts above the revelry, "You guys have this festival every year?"

"Sure," Gary shrugs. "Long as I can remember."

"It's fun!" Annie sings out, followed by a bellowing, "Yee Haw!"

She grabs Gary's hand as she twirls herself one way, then the other. Out of the crowd Dave, Tony, and Zack Stikker materialize. They have located Gary. The boys exchange high fives. "We were looking all over for you!" Dave calls out.

"I told you that I'd be by the pulled pork sandwiches and here I am," Gary shrugs.

"Pulled pork," Zach inhales deeply. "I love that stuff."

Zach is fourteen years old and one of the youngest Teeners new to the team this year. He is Dave's neighbor and good friend. Years of playing backyard ball with his older friend has made Zach a pretty decent ballplayer. He has found a starting spot at second base as the year progressed.

"You guys wait here. I'm going to get a pulled pork sammich," Zach waves at his teammates as he walks to the booth selling BBQ pork.

"We'll wait for ya," Dave calls behind Zach.

Annie stops dancing and leans on Gary wrapping her arms around his shoulder.

Dave frowns at Gary watching Annie draped over him," I don't imagine you'd like to join us."

"What's up? What do you have in mind?" Gary smiles curiously.

"We're huntin'. We've located the herd; now we're puttin' the stalk on."

Dave points to a group of female high school classmates and other young ladies from adjacent communities huddled a few hundred feet away.

"Ah, I see," Gary nods. "I wish I could come with ya, but I've already been tagged by this one."

Gary pulls Annie closer and kisses the top of her head. "Yeah, it was a bit like Wild Kingdom. She shot me with a tranquilizer dart, and the next thing I know I got this big radio collar around my neck tracking my every move." Gary holds out a fine braided silver chain around his neck, a gift from Annie.

"Oh, ha-ha," Annie smirks. "You loved it." She slaps Gary's butt.

"Ouch," Gary cries out. "No hitting."

Zach returns to the group, gulping down his sandwich. Gary turns his attention back to Tony and Dave, "So, at least you guys are giving them a sporting chance...you know...bringing Tony along. He's like woman repellent."

Tony pats down his hair, "I am f-f-f-feeling lucky tonight."

Gary holds his hand to his ear. "Shhh. Did you hear that? Some girl just screamed. She's realizing that her desperate attempt for company may leave her no choice but Tony."

Tony smirks, "The Tonester d-d-doesn't mind a p-p-pity hand job."

Dave cocks his head, "How cute. And which hand of yours will the Tonester be using tonight? His left hand or his right hand?"

Tony shakes his head in disgust, reaches deep into his right front pocket, and digs around. "H-h-hey, D-D-D-Dave, I got something for y-y-y-you right here in my p-p-p-pocket." Tony pulls his hand out of his pocket with his middle finger extended and waves it in front of Dave's face. "Y-Y-Y-You can keep it," Tony stutters. "In f-f-f-fact, I have one in my l-l-l-left pocket too." Tony digs his hand into his left pocket and pulls out his hand with his middle finger extended. "K-k-k-keep them both."

Dave laughs, "With pleasure." He grabs Tony's left middle finger and quickly bends it back driving Tony to his knee.

"U-U-U-Uncle!" Tony cries out.

Dave lets go and Tony stands and brushes off his pants, "Son of a bitch. L-L-Let's go! Time's a-wasting!"

Dave waves, "Later,"

Gary gives a nod to the departing trio, "See ya later."

Dave turns back around, "Not if we can help it." He bounces his eyebrows, "Wish us luck!"

"Good luck!" Gary shouts to the guys as they disappear into the crowd, heading toward the girls.

Gary pulls Annie close then pushes her away as she twirls in the ever increasing mass of people closing in on them. He pulls her back to his side, "What do you say? Should we try to get up by the stage and dance?"

"Sure!" Annie pulls on Gary, heading toward the stage, but she snaps back as Gary doesn't move.

"You know what?" Gary asks. "I think," he inhales deeply, "that we need to have one more pulled pork sandwich before we leave our prime spot."

Annie smiles and shakes her head, "Fine."

Chapter 24
Apply Yourself

At 9:00 a.m. sharp the doorbell rings at Gary's house. Not that Gary hears the gong. He is still asleep in his bedroom in the basement, far from any noise or disturbance. Gary's mom, Mary Hillmann, answers the door. Forty-year old Mary with her petite frame and short cropped hair opens the door to find Annie holding a pair of shoes. "Hi, Annie. Please come in," Mary invites as she escorts the young girl to the kitchen. "Gary's still asleep, but I'll go get him up. You guys were out pretty late, but it's time for him to get up."

"No, no. I just wanted to drop off his stuff. Gary left his shoes in my car when he put his boots on. He thought he could dance better in his cowboy boots than his basketball shoes."

Annie holds up a pair of white, leather high-top Addidas basketball shoes. "Oh yeah?" Mary questions. "How did it go?" She points to the floor, "Just set the shoes down anywhere."

Annie drops the shoes and pushes them against the wall. Annie smiles and answers the question, "As it turns out, he can't dance in any footwear."

Mary laughs, "Like his father I would bet. They think they can dance, but to call it dancing would be a stretch." Mary sweeps her hand to the counter. Three stools line a countertop eating area. "Please, have a seat at the bar. I'll go get Gary up."

Annie sits and looks at the headlines of the morning paper while she waits. In a moment Mary returns. She moves to the refrigerator, "Did you want some orange juice?"

"Sure," Annie accepts the offer, and Mary pours a glass of juice for her.

"Gary will be right up."

Annie sips her juice, "Did you go to the dance last night?"

Mary nods, "We went for an hour or so. Harry is golfing in some tournament this weekend in Brayton. He had to be there early, so we didn't stay out late."

Gary emerges from the basement a little bleary-eyed and blinks at the bright, sunny kitchen. His mom pours him a glass of juice, and he swallows most of it finally acknowledging Annie with a hand on her shoulder. "Hey, what are you doing here?"

Annie points to the shoes in the corner, "You left your shoes in the car. I didn't know if you'd need them right away."

"Oh, thanks. That's nice of you. How come you're not working?"

Mary interrupts, "Yikes, speaking of work, I have to head up to the church. We're hosting the festival pancake breakfast tomorrow morning, and we need to get set up."

Mary grabs her purse and car keys, "You guys are going to be there tomorrow, aren't you?"

She doesn't wait for an answer and starts out the door, but stops and comes back to the dining area next to the kitchen. From an antique roll-top desk opposite the serving counter, she produces a large envelope. "I almost forgot," Mary tosses the envelope on the counter. "Here is the final registration packet for Kirtland Prep Academy. You need to fill it out right away."

The envelope spins in front of Annie finally stopping, so she can see the embossed return address. She stares at the envelope not comprehending the conversation going on around her. "See you later. Bye, Annie," Mary calls out, disappearing out the door in a rush.

Mary's comment begins to sink in with Annie. She lifts a heavy finger with all her strength. She traces her finger of the school crest and embossed Olde English lettering on the return address.

"I-I-I don't understand," Annie stammers. "You're leaving Reedville?" Annie slouches in her seat, her world spins.

Gary grimaces, "I was going to tell you, but I was waiting for a better time."

A tear runs down Annie's cheek, and she wipes at it and misses as it falls to the counter. "When? When is the best time to break my heart?"

"I'm sorry. I should have told you." Gary sighs, "This is very important to me. This prep school may get me into the best universities in the world. I told you I want to go to Pepperdine. My uncle went there."

"I can't believe this," Annie shakes her head in disbelief. Another tear traces her cheek to her chin.

"I can't..." her voice trails away, and she struggles to get to her feet, pushing out of the stool against the counter. "I just..." She wipes at the stream of tears and looks at her hand in disbelief at the teardrops. Her face produces a smile of shock at her own foolishness. "I was just telling Uncle Marv and Aunt April that I would like to stay here for the school year. They said they would talk to my parents."

Gary moves to try to console Annie. She pushes him away brusquely. "Don't! Don't you dare," She hisses.

Annie turns and heads for the door. "Annie!" Gary calls after her.

She runs to the door, sobs rack her body as she covers her eyes and the full onslaught of grief overtakes her. She opens the door and exits, slamming the door behind her.

Chapter 25
Mediator

A rare 11:00 a.m. abbreviated batting practice is held to accommodate the coaches' schedules. Coach Boots is on his way to an amateur game, and Coach Willis has a doctor's appointment. Each player is given a dozen swings and that is the practice. It is a warm and humid morning about to turn into a dog day afternoon. Corn growing weather is the phrase people in the area liked to use. Not a breath of wind, no cloud in the sky; nothing but sunshine, heat, and humidity. If you are lucky enough to be standing next to a corn field in such weather, you can hear the corn grow. In the parking lot next to the practice field Gary and Dave trudge across the gravel surface to their vehicles. "It's gonna be a hot one today," Dave announces.

"Thank you, Captain Obvious," Gary mocks. "It's already fuckin' boiling."

Dave laughs, "Well, what do you say? Ya wanna hit the pool straight away?"

Gary wipes the sweat from his brow and tosses his gear into the back of his truck. "I can't. Annie will be there."

"Yeah, she's a…" Dave sighs and drops his duffle next to the door of his car. Dave leans against his little Ford Fiesta, and it groans, pushing back against his weight, "Oh, please…don't tell me…"

Gary kicks off his spiked shoe from his left foot and hops around as he attempts to put on his hi-top basketball shoe. He quickly gives up and steps down in the dirty, gravelly parking lot. "Why is it so fucking hot?" he curses.

Gary kicks off his other spiked shoe and dons a basketball shoe. Dave stands staring at his friend, "You guys broke up? That's what's put you in this mood."

Dave leans over with a groan and unties his spikes. He rummages through his bag for some shoes. Gary falls back against his truck shaking his head in disbelief, "She found out I was going to leave for prep school and flipped out. She won't return my calls."

Dave locates a pair of flip-flops in his bag and tosses them on the ground. He kicks off a spiked shoe and struggles to peel his sock off. Gary watches, somewhat bemused and smiles at the battle. Finally conquering one flip-flop, Dave works on the other foot. Eventually straightening his back in victory with a groan, he gasps for breath and mops his brow with a dirty sock. Gary laughs at the final indignity of Dave sopping his sweat with his sock. Dave stows his gear with a gasping breath and meets Gary's eyes, "You want me to talk to her?" Dave asks.

"Psssh," Gary reacts disgustedly. "I'm not sure what she thought was going to happen. The way she reacted, you'd thought we were engaged to be married."

"I'll talk to her," Dave resolutely states.

"I dunno," Gary shakes his head, "it probably won't do much good." Dave shrugs, "It can't hurt."

* * * * *

The crowded swimming pool reflects the heat of the afternoon. Wall to wall kids splash and jump shoulder to shoulder. The shrill screams of adolescent boys and girls pierce the air. It is a headache in the making for lifeguards on their perches. Umbrellas overhead shield the sun for the sentries in charge of the pool, but the heat is still oppressive. Annie is guarding the deep end on this rotation. She sits on her chair, scanning the water as kids fly off the diving boards into the water. Her sunglasses reflect the scene in the pool below her. Annie holds her whistle hooked to a lanyard and twirls it wrapping around her finger clockwise, then spinning it the other way where the whistle coils around her extended digit counter-clockwise.

The deep end of the pool with the diving boards, although more intimidating to look at from a civilian's perspective, is more organized than any other part of the pool. The low dive and the high dive are parallel, and only one swimmer is on each board at a time. It is orderly in that one person is on the diving board and one in the pool, and the next person cannot leap from the board until the person having just jumped reaches the edge of the pool and the exit ladder. The high dive is about seven feet high and the low dive is about two feet up. A steady stream of swimmers rotates in and out of the pool using the diving boards. The rules are clear, and kids wait in line for their turn to spring off the boards. In and out of the pool they circle dripping with water as they exit the pool and get right back in line for their next flight into the twelve foot depths of the blue water of the deep end.

An amazing variety of leaps from diving boards can be observed. The most common method used for going from board to water is the running flailing leap. Kids run as fast as they can and sail as far as their momentum will take them before splashing down into blue. Off the high dive, many jumpers step off the board and "toothpick" into the water. They try to stay as vertical as possible and slip into the water as cleanly as they can without a splash. Their momentum will take them to the bottom of the pool and they can push off the pool floor and back to the surface. Then there are the splashers, the "can opener." This jumper leaps off the board holding one leg to his chest and leans just a bit to produce a splash. Another favorite to provide a directional deluge to an unsuspecting person on deck is the "preacher." The swimmer jumps off, covers his face with his hands like he is holding a Bible to his nose, and leans, aligning his back to the target of his splash. The most famous splasher is the "cannon ball." Everyone knows this one, jump off the board, hug both knees to your chest, yell out "cannon ball," and enter the water butt first for a tremendous splash.

Putting a good splash on a lifeguard always gets attention and likely a "timeout" or even a suspension from the pool. Dave climbed the high dive and weighed his options, deciding on the cannonball. He executes it to perfection, and, as he emerges from under the water, he hears the trill of the whistle, knowing it is meant for him. "Dave," Annie shouts down from her chair.

Dave treads water a moment and finally swims toward the ladder, "Hey, Annie, how'd ya like my cannonball?"

"Out of the pool, Dave," Annie barks.

The whistle momentarily pushes a pause button on the activities in the pool as kids look to see what has happened and who may be in trouble. Satisfied that someone is being punished, the screams and splashes resume. Dave dog paddles to the edge of the pool and climbs the ladder to the deck. He sweeps his dripping hair back over his head and looks up at Annie in her chair as he leans on the elevated seat. Annie does not look down, she resumes twirling her whistle around her finger. Her expression is stoic as she scans the pool. "Hi, Dave," she finally speaks without looking down.

Dave stands dripping wet below her. A small puddle of water has formed at his feet and grows, expanding on the warm concrete deck. Dave smiles, taking in Annie's tan, tone body. She wears a bikini swimsuit exposing as much bare skin as possible, and Dave enjoys the view above him. "Love the white, zinc on your nose. It really suits you," Dave touches his nose and points to Annie.

Annie does not look down, and she continues to turn her head back and forth, slowly scanning the pool. "Gary says 'Hi'," Dave offers.

Annie takes a quick look down at Dave, punctuated with a frown, before she turns her attention back to observing the pool.

Annie continues to stare out over the screaming, splashing kids before her. Finally she speaks sarcastically, "What are you, his messenger-boy now?"

"Nope, just a good-will ambassador."

Annie twirls the whistle even faster now in anger as she listens to Dave. "Gary told me this wouldn't work, but I insisted it couldn't hurt," Dave puts his hands up in defense. "I'm here on my own account. Because he's my friend."

"I don't need an ambassador," Annie barks without looking down.

Dave shifts his weight and leans heavily on the stanchion of the chair. "Listen, Annie. How do you think I felt when I found out he might leave? He didn't even tell me! I'm his best friend!" Dave points both hands to his chest. "He never said one word to me; Gary's mom said something to my mom. That's how I found out."

Two kids to the right of Annie wrestle in the pool; she blows her whistle, "Stuart! Mikey!" she yells. "You are out of the pool until the break! I warned you once already!"

The ten-year old boys swim to the edge of the pool and begrudgingly climb out on the deck. They move past Annie. "How long 'til break?" Stuart asks as they pass.

"It's only ten minutes away," Annie counsels.

The boys nod, satisfied the punishment isn't too harsh. They move to an empty spot on the warm concrete and lay down on their stomachs pressing themselves against the warm concrete side by side. With their arms at their sides, they look like a couple of skinny white sea lions as they pick their heads up to acknowledge their friends mocking them from the pool.

"Like I said, how do you think I felt? Gary and I have been best friends since we were born, and he never said 'boo' to me about leaving."

After a full minute of silence, Annie speaks without looking down, "If he can't share important things with people that care about him, that's his problem. He can deal with it himself."

There is more silence. Annie looks down at Dave, "Why is he like that?"

Dave shrugs and continues to shrug at the end of every sentence, "He's just that way. I guess he doesn't want a lot of drama. Or he doesn't want to hurt people's feelings. Maybe he doesn't want to get hurt himself."

Dave shakes his head and holds up his hands, "I guess it's a defense mechanism."

Annie doesn't respond, continuing to stare out across the pool as she shakes her head slowly side to side.

"Anyway," Dave continues. "You don't see me shunning him for this, and I don't think you should either. He's a good guy."

Dave steps back from the chair, "Well, I'm going to go." Dave turns and slowly walks away.

Annie blows her whistle and yells, "Dave! No running!"

Dave turns around with a quizzical look on his face. Annie finally smiles ever so slightly and waves Dave off. Dave's expression of surprise morphs into a smile. He waves, turns, and continues to head to the locker room.

Gregory L. Heitmann

Chapter 26
Totaled

    The regular season is winding down, and the only games left are tournaments. First is the conference tournament. Spirits are high after winning the regular season conference championship and receiving the number one seed for the tournament. The number one seeding brings a bye for the first round, thus the team is afforded an additional day of rest. As always, the day off brings an uneasy feeling to Coach Willis. A day off does nothing but break momentum in his book. Following this logic it may be a day off from a game, but there is still practice to try to stay in the routine of playing baseball every day. After the final early morning practice of the year produces a crisp result, the team is released early. Players mill about in the parking lot, not sure what to do with a couple extra hours before the swimming pool opens. Going home is not considered a real option, so they hang in the parking lot, leaning on cars, shooting the breeze, and noting the cool morning air, a refreshing change from the usual late-afternoon-heat-of-the-day practice times.

    The cottonwood trees that line the parking lot tower overhead. Their leaves rustle a soothing whisper in the wind. Gary and Dave lean on their vehicles and chat. They both unknowingly smile and soak in the morning. The sun is gaining altitude, but the shade from the giant cottonwoods keeps the vehicles in shadows. "How's your hamstring?" Gary asks.

    Dave flexes his leg, "I'm sure it will be fine."

    Dave and Gary still loiter, not even changing out of their spikes yet. Their attention is drawn to the roar of a revving car engine, and the two glance over at Aric's Camaro. He has fired it up and is demonstrating to a few members of the team his recently upgraded exhaust system. According to his calculations, he will get an additional ten horsepower from the premium muffler and tailpipes. The revving engine roars up and down as Aric works the throttle.

    The short respite in the refuge of the parking lot is over. The pleasant interlude of enjoying a moment of solitude before the mounting pressure of the tournaments has come and gone. The serenity is further evaporated by the incessant engine whine. The throttle roar is followed by the throaty rumble of Aric's hot rod at idle.

The page of summer turns. The end of the baseball season, the end of summer break from school, the end of an era of friendships had been suspended in the peaceful morning parking lot gathering, but now the moment has passed.

Zach pulls up to Gary and Dave, riding his mo-ped, an early edition of a motorized bicycle that you pedaled to start and a small gas motor that would kick-in to assist your pedal-power. Zach has his duffle slung over his back, and, in between the racing engine interruptions, he asks his question, "Hey, guys. What time does the bus leave for the tournament tomorrow?"

Gary fields the question, "Be at April's at 9:45…in the morning."

This draws a laugh from Dave, who adds with a harsh emphasis on the a.m. arrival time, "We leave at 10…in the morning."

"Sounds good," Zach nods, shifting the duffle on his back.

Zach pushes forward on his mo-ped, pedaling furiously before flicking the switch and getting motor assistance. The revving engine drowns out the whine of the mo-ped, followed by a lull, then a roar again, but this time with the added grittiness of tires spinning on gravel. Aric spins out backward from his parking spot into Zach's path. The mo-ped swerves, but Zach is unable to avoid the Camaro. He crashes into the back end of Aric's car, splintering the tail light as well as gouging and denting the brand new car.

"Oh my God!" Dave calls out at he runs to help Zach quickly followed by Gary.

Aric is out of the car in a flash standing over Zach yelling, "What the hell are you doing? My car!"

Dave reaches Zach and kneels down beside him. He is already in tears holding his arm. Aric is in a fit, "You dented my car!"

He kneels and inspects the damage, picking up red and orange shards of plastic. "I don't believe this! You dipshit!" Aric glares menacingly at Zach before resuming his collection of plastic splinters.

Gary straightens from his stooped position over Zach and turns his attention from the injured boy to Aric. He glares at Aric and stands over the kneeling boy, "You're the dipshit, asshole. You're worried about your stupid car?"

Aric stands hesitatingly as he looks at Zach still seated in the gravel, sobbing and rocking in pain as he holds his wrist. Gary shoves Aric back against the car, "You coulda killed him!"

Aric raises his hands, "Take it easy, Gary. I'm sorry."

Gary gives Aric another shove, forcing him to stumble back against the car. "You're sorry? Tell it to the cops, douche bag. I'm calling the police."

Zach interrupts as he stands gingerly, "It's ok. I'm all right."

Gary gestures to the broken bike, "Look at your mo-ped. It's totaled!"

Aric steps forward with hands in surrender, talking a mile-a-minute, "No, no, don't worry about it; I'll get Zach a new mo-ped. You're right it was my fault. I'll take care of everything. We don't need the cops."

Dave intervenes, "Come on, Zach. I'll get you home."

Dave escorts Zach to his car. Gary questions him, "Are you sure you're ok?"

"It was just an accident," Zach wipes at his tears. "Uh, I got to get my bag."

Zach breaks from Dave and goes to pick up his duffle bag separated from his shoulder during the crash. He reaches to pick up the bag, but winces. "Damn it!" He cries in pain. "My wrist!"

Dave moves to grab the duffle, and he throws the bag in the back seat as Zach loads himself into the car. Dave gets in and looks over at his passenger, "Dang! Look at your wrist. It's swelling like crazy."

Gary leans in to Dave's window, "I'll get the mo-ped loaded up in my truck and hauled over to Zach's."

"Look at his wrist," Dave gestures with a thumb.

"Oh, boy," Gary shakes his head. "Get him home."

Dave backs out and spins out of the parking lot, swerving around the mo-ped. Gary moves toward the shattered bike. He points at Aric and scowls, "You, help me get this thing loaded into my truck."

Aric hustles over to Gary, and they lift the bent and battered mo-ped into the back of Gary's truck. Aric shuts the tailgate. "I cant' believe this. My dad is going to kill me for denting the car. Why did I do this? I was just dicking around like he always says. Shit."

Aric looks around, noticing for the first time the pale, scared expressions of his teammates. They have witnessed the frightening event and stood by in shock, frozen and doing nothing to assist their injured teammate. He forces a weak smile as he looks at Chuck, Turner, and

Jesse, searching for a sympathetic indication from anyone. "Live and learn," he finally shrugs.

Gary doesn't respond. He looks at Aric and shakes his head as he gets into his truck and pulls out of the parking lot.

Chapter 27
Tony, Tonie, Tonee

    Tournament time brings a tension to the bus as it is loaded. Coach Boots sits uncomfortably in the driver's seat, ready to go a half hour before the scheduled departure time. He is nervous and greets each player with the same twitchy nod of the head as each one steps onto the bus. Coach Willis sits in the front seat, reading the Brayton Daily Times, oblivious to players or the nervousness of his assistant coach. The conference tournament is meaningless in the pursuit of a state championship. Sure it is another notch in your belt or a trophy on the shelf of City Hall, but as far as a state championship goes, it is worthless. The real test is the regional tourney, and, if you win that, you advance to state.

    Zach shows up at five minutes to ten. He is dressed in jeans and a t-shirt. Most notably he carries his jersey in his hand. He doesn't have a duffle bag, instead he sports a lily white cast on his wrist. "Oh, my God! You broke your wrist!" Gary cries out as Zach makes his way down the aisle of the bus. Everyone turns their attention to Zach briefly as he holds up the offending limb. The interest in Zach is momentary, as Aric becomes the object of derision. Hats, gloves, and full duffle bags fly in Aric's direction, some landing with authority. "Ouch! It was an accident! Ow!" Aric cries as the deluge of disdain rains down on him, accompanied by every curse imaginable.

    The bus waits for Chuck. It is not unusual for Chuck to show up at the last minute; in fact, it has become the norm. Today Chuck is later than usual. Coach Willis has gone into the café to call Chuck's house and see if he is on his way. After a few moments Coach Willis ambles back to the bus from April's Café and climbs aboard. He taps Coach Booth on the back, "Let's go." He moves to his seat and announces, "Chuck's not going to make it. I just talked to his step-dad, and they are in the middle of the wheat harvest and field work."

    A murmur goes through the bus before a shout from J.W. rings out, "That's bullshit! My dad let me go, and we're doing the same thing!"

"Take it easy!" Coach Willis orders as he flops down in his seat. He taps Coach Booth on the shoulder again, "We'll be fine. Come on, Bootsy, fire her up and let's go."

Coach Boots swings around the driver's seat facing forward, starts the bus, and they roll out of the parking lot, easing onto the highway. The Reedville Teeners begins the tournament season two starters short.

* * * * *

In the back of the bus, the players lean toward the aisle and the makeshift poker table, a thirty-two quart cooler. It is a Reedville tradition for Teener players and above to enjoy nickel and dime poker on the road trips. The card game is a distraction for the solemn mood of tourney time, added to the loss of two starting players. "Oh, Christ!" Tony howls as he throws down his cards on the cooler, "F-f-f-fixed! That game was fixed!"

Gary's winning smile, as he rakes the nickels and dimes from the pot into his hat, fades as Tony's cards bounce off the cooler and off Gary's shoulder. "Take it easy!" Gary glares at Tony.

"I-i-i-it's gotta be f-f-f-fixed!" Tony stutters.

Gary mimics Tony's stuttering, "T-T-T-T-Tony! Y-Y-Y-Y-You should be f-f-f-fixed. I have a recurring nightmare; a herd of fat baby Tonies roaming the streets, devouring all the food in sight."

A chortle rises from the bus. An annoyed Tony is in no mood; he stands, "Y-y-y-ya want some of this? B-b-b-bring it on!"

"Luckily for all of us," Gary waves Tony away, "nobody wants any of that. Thus, thankfully, we are not in danger of little Tonies."

Raucous laughter fills the bus.

Dave nods and seriously intones, "It is true."

"Shut up, Dave!" Tony snaps, "st-st-st-stay out of this. This is between me and Gary."

Dave puts his hands up in surrender, leaning away from a frothing Tony. "Whatever, dude."

Gary points at Tony and says, "Sit!" as if ordering a dog. "Let's play cards. I'm in no mood for a 'sick off.' Unbunch your panties, Tony, and just relax."

Tony sits slowly back down and mockingly questions, "Sc-Sc-Sc-Scared?"

Gary laughs at the thought of being frightened of Tony, "I just don't want to go up against your big family."

A look of bewilderment crosses Tony's face. Gary points at Tony, "You got you, Tony-Tone-Tonester."

Gary searches the bus, looking around, finally pointing at Fitz, "You got Tony-Twin, a slovenly version of you."

Gary reaches over and slaps a hand on Dave's shoulder, "You got Tony-Twin version two...sorry Dave."

Dave winces at the comment, "Hey!"

Gary makes a bemused face of innocence, "I said 'sorry.' You're kinda the same proportion as Tony,"

Gary puffs out his cheeks and holds his arms out to indicate a rotund roundness.

The laughs start getting bigger from the crowd drawn around Gary as he checks off the list of Tonies. Fin is next. Gary stabs a finger in Fin's direction, "Then there's Fin...the multiple-monikered-Tony. Let's see, he will answer to Tony-Twitch, the Spastic Tony, and even Ghost-Tony."

"Ghost-Tony?" Fin questions overhearing the conversation.

"You know," Gary continues. "Because of your albino like appearance?"

Laughter ripples through the seats. "Let's see...Who's next?" Gary examines the crowd. "Oh, yeah. The little guys." Gary points to Jesse. "You got Jesse, Tony-Dick, the little guy representing your micro-penis."

Even Tony can't keep his faux stern expression in place, letting loose a laugh. Gary gives a nod toward Turner, "Don't forget Tony-Smell. The odor is a constant reminder. Hey, Tony-Smell, you ever shower?"

Gary finally levels a pointed finger pistol at Aric. "Last, but not least, the Toniest of them all, Tony-King, a.k.a., Tony-Douche!"

Aric stands and bows, accepting the boisterous laughter. Gary shakes his head, "Aric, what can I say? You are the Toniest of the Tonies...and I don't mean that in a good way."

Aric nods and bows again. Tony forces a frown, trying not to laugh, "Hey, I can't say that doesn't hurt my feelings. B-b-b-b-but, you forgot you! Y-y-y-you...you are Tony-Sick. Y-y-y-you got the sickest, gutter mind out of anyone I know."

Gary laughs and holds up a hand, and Tony high fives him. "I guess we'll call it a draw."

From the backseat of the bus, the song "Girl You Know It's True" by Milli Vanilli emanates from the stereo. "Crank it, Lawrence!" a voice cries out.

Lawrence twists the volume to distortion level on the boombox. "These guys are going to be bigger than the Beatles!"

Gary laughs and shouts over the music, "Yeah, we'll probably have a President like them too!"

Lawrence's eyes widen, "You think we'll have a Black President?"

Gary shakes his head, "That's called sarcasm, son."

Lawrence is unphased. He busts his best Milli Vanilli moves; mimicking the video of their dance moves he has seen a million times.

All eyes are on Lawrence until Gary interrupts, "Can we get back to playing some cards? I need a little more money for the concession stand when we get to Clarkston."

Chapter 28
Defeat

As bad as the day begins, with two starters out of the conference tournament, it just seems to go downhill from there. Trent, the starting pitcher for the opening game, the ace of the pitching staff, makes it through one-third of an inning. He walks five out of the first six hitters and is relieved of pitching duties due to a blister on the index finger of this throwing hand.

In the course of the coaches' discussion on the pitching rotation, and who should relieve Trent, Coach Willis sums it up, "The rotation don't mean nothin' if we don't win this game."

Trent moves to shortstop, shifting Aric to left field when Gary comes in to pitch. Gary manages to get the last two outs in the first inning, but not before he hits a batter and walks three more hitters on top of giving up two line drive singles. When all is said and done for the first inning, it is seven to zero Clarkston beating down the Reedville powerhouse.

By the fourth inning Clarkston's lead grows to nine to nothing, but Reedville has finally mounted a threat with runners at first and second, nobody out. Gary steps to the plate, and the Reedville dugout has some life. Whooping and hollering pours out of the dugout. Phrases indicting the Clarkston pitcher's mother's virtue spew forth, causing Coach Willis to move from this third base coaching box next to the dugout screen to chastise the team. The lecturing over, Coach is back in the third base coaching box.

Gary digs into the batter's box, finally feeling comfortable. He takes a couple more practice swings and waits as the pitcher strolls around the mound, rubbing the ball and gathering himself against the first offensive challenge of the game. Before the pitcher puts his foot on the pitching rubber, Gary hears Coach Willis yell from the third base coaching box, "Hillmann! Hillmann! Hey, G Mann!"

Gary calls time out and steps out of the batter's box, looking down at his coach. Coach Willis is rubbing his arms, touching his face, wiping his thigh, in random order finally finishing with a thumb and fore finger pinching the bill of his hat. Gary sighs. There is no play on, he thought, until Coach Willis claps his hands, steps back in the coach's box, and grabs his belt buckle. "Oh, Christ," Gary whispers to himself. "Not the bunt sign."

Gary shakes his head side to side as he looks at the coach, denying the sign. Coach Willis emphatically grabs at his buckle. The ump finally intervenes, "Batter up!"

Gary continues to shake his head as he steps into the box. "Come on, Hillmann, get a hit now," Coach Willis calls out with a clap of his hands.

Coach Boots in the first base coach's box echoes Coach Willis with a loud series of claps. "Hustle now!" he cries out.

The Clarkston pitcher stretches, checks the runner at second base, and delivers the pitch home. Gary squares to bunt, and the base runners take off. The pitch is high, and Gary pops the ball straight back to the pitcher on a little blooping liner. The pitcher catches the ball chest high. Coach Boots screams, piercing the air, "Baaaackk! Baaaacccck! Get Back!"

It is too late. For an unknown reason, the runners bolt on the pitch; not waiting to be sure the bunt is on the ground. Gary never makes a step out of the box before the bunt is nabbed out of the air. The pitcher turns and fires the ball to the shortstop covering second base. He touches the base and flips the ball sidearm to the first baseman, completing the triple play and squashing the Reedville rally in one fell swoop. The Clarkston dugout is in a frenzy, cheering and spilling out of the dugout high fiving the players coming in from their defensive positions.

Gary stands in shock holding his hands on his helmet; fingers interlocked looking in disbelief at the celebrating Clarkston players. Coach Boots jogs by shooting a look for Gary. A look that could kill. "Show some hustle, Hillmann! Get back to the dugout."

All the life is sucked out of the Reedville Teeners. They are as flat as they have played all year. Finally scratching across two runs in the bottom of the sixth inning gets Gary to the plate again with a shot at leaving on a more positive note. With nobody on he takes a pitch for a strike. Two hefty swings and misses later he strikes out for the third out of the inning. Gary's frustration with himself explodes when Coach Boots jogs by, returning to the dugout from his post in the first base coaching box, "Hustle," Boots scowls as he passes Gary.

Gary flips the bat aside and rips the Velcro open on his batting gloves as he mutters to himself, staring at the scoreboard. He flips his helmet toward the bat rack, and the helmet springs high in the air. Propelled by landing perfectly on an earflap, the batting helmet bounces, end over end, vaulting over the dugout. Gary stops and watches the flight of the helmet sailing through the air. It all seems in slow motion. Coach Boots has had enough. He is in full view of Gary's tantrum and helmet toss, and this is more than he can bear. "Lawrence, you're in for Hillmann! You're done, Hillmann; grab some bench."

"What else could go wrong?" Gary mutters to himself as he pulls his batting gloves off and finds a seat on the bench. Lawrence hustles to find his hat and glove and runs out of the dugout, but not before finding Gary and providing a fist bump of acknowledgement then sprinting to left field.

In the dugout Gary finds a seat next to Coach Willis. He flops down beside the coach who sits with his arms folded; realizing defeat is imminent. Gary leans forward head in hands, elbows on his knees. He knows he was wrong and offers a simple apology to the coach, "Sorry, Coach."

Coach Willis waves away the apology with a grunt, "Bleaaah."

He drops a heavy hand on Gary's knee, gives his knee a shake, and ends the affectionate gesture with three solid pats on Gary's leg. All is forgiven from Coach Willis' standpoint; Coach Boots, well, that is another story.

Fin is in to pitch the end of the game as they finish out the top of the sixth inning. Fin does a good job in relief for the struggling Reedville pitching staff. Unfortunately, the defense doesn't rise to the occasion quite as well. J.W. is in at second base, substituting for Zach and his broken wrist. Fin lays in a good pitch to the Clarkston hitter, busting him inside. The batter fists a looping fly ball to second base. J.W. staggers under the ball, and he drops the easy popup. Compounding his mistake, he spins to pick up the escaping ball and attempts to get the runner hustling to first base. J.W. stumbles and flips the ball high into the crowd. Putting icing on his cake of embarrassment he continues to lose his balance and ends his seemingly drunken choreography by falling on his face.

From the dugout Coach Willis stands and tries to offer encouragement, "That's ok, J.W.!"

Coach Willis claps his hands and returns to the bench, mumbling in disgust to no one in particular inside the dugout, "Jesus, J.W. Can't catch, can't throw...can't hit. Can't run...balls are too big...dick's too short."

The players on the bench try to hide their quiet snickering. It's no matter to Coach Willis; he is oblivious. "Bootsy!" Coach Willis calls out, not even looking to the end of the bench where Coach Boots leans against the railing. "Didn't I ask you earlier this year to play J.W. more to see if he could handle it?"

"Yeah," Coach Boots replies.

"Does it look like he can handle it?" Coach Willis punctuates his question with a spit of tobacco juice on the dugout floor.

"No, Coach," Boots replies with all the animation of a corpse.

"Well, Jesus Christ," Coach Willis spits again. "We need to figure something out. Who's gonna replace Zach and his broken wrist? Goddam Regions are next week!"

"I'm on it coach," Boots replies in a monotone.

"How 'bout Lawrence at second base, coach?" Gary speaks up. "He hustles, and he's got a good glove and attitude. I think he'd pick it up no problem. Remember when he filled in for Dave at catcher up in Rock Lake?"

Coach Willis looks at Gary then down to the end of the bench where Coach Boots sits. "Hey, Boots, talk to Lawrence and give him some ground balls at second."

"Will do, Coach," Boots acknowledges with a nod.

The inning ends with the score ten to two. In Reedville's final at bat two ground outs bring Dave to bat as the final hurrah.

Dave digs in, and the final rally cry from the dugout sounds from Reedville, "Give 'er a ride, Dave!" Coach Willis encourages from the bench, having turned over his third base coaching position to Boots while Trent fills in at the first base coaching box. Just like that Dave watches two strikes sail across the plate thigh high, and down the middle. Cheers turn to groans in the dugout. Coach Willis' chatter is not as positive as it was, "Come on, Dave! Watcha waitin' for? A lollipop?"

The snickering in the dugout ripples through from end to end. When Marv whips out the lollipop line, you know he's aggravated. The final pitch is an eye-high fastball that Dave can't lay off. He strikes out for the final out of the game, ending the hope of a Reedville Conference Championship.

"That's ok, Dave," Coach Willis calls out from the dugout as Dave, lumbers back to the bench.

Coach Boots is already back at the dugout rail, leaning over and looking down at the players in disgust. "Bootsy!" Coach Willis calls. Coach Booth snaps his head to look at the coach. "Can we get some hitting help for Dave?"

"Will do, Coach," Boots intones. "Get over and shake their hands!" orders Coach Boots. "Then get your butts back here and get this gear bagged up. We're gonna get outta here."

The teams meet at home plate and go through the line, exchanging high fives, hand shakes, and meaningless comments of "good game."

Sacking the equipment is a solemn event, and once the bus is loaded the reality of defeat has squelched any sign of revelry. Coach Boots starts the bus and drives forward about fifty feet before stopping and turning off the engine. He gets up from the driver's seat and moves down the aisle to address the team. "I am embarrassed. You call that an effort out there today?" He meets the eyes of all players staring back at him from their seats. "I am utterly embarrassed. I have never seen such a weak effort from any Reedville team in all my years of baseball."

Coach Boots points to Gary. "Bunting into a triple-play. F-u-u-u-u-u-u-uck," he drawls stretching the last word out as a doctor would ask a patient to say "Ahhhh."

Coach Boots shakes his head in disgust. "Might as well hand it over to them on a silver platter."

Coach Boots returns to the driver's seat, starts the engine, and points the bus towards home. Two miles go by and the team still sits quietly until Gary sighs, nodding his head in earnest, "Wow. A truly inspirational speech."

The tension is broken. Gary claps his hands together, "Let's play some cards! Lawrence…tunes….please!"

The boom box fires up, and Warrant's song "Cherry Pie" blares while players sing along.

Gregory L. Heitmann

Chapter 29
Announcement

It is the definition of mixed emotions for Gary as he emerges from his basement bedroom in the morning. He is still sickened by the previous night's loss. He never had any doubts that they would win the state championship, repeating the feat as so many of the Reedville Teener teams had done before. But now, it is there. A hint of doubt rattles through his brain. Maybe this is the year that marks the end of the glory days for the Teeners. The mail has arrived and is in a neat stack on the counter, right next to where he places his box of Frosted Flakes cereal, bowl, and milk. The letters and magazines stare at him. It is the large envelope on the bottom of the pile that he grabs first. The overstuffed white enveloped bears the Kirtland Academy emblem embossed on the return address. Gary slices open the envelope, and a class catalog emblazoned with the emblem superimposed on the scenic Sandia Mountains of Albuquerque on its cover slides from the correspondence. Clipped to the catalog is a formal letter that begins with the words, "Congratulations and Welcome!"

A feeling of nostalgia and melancholy come over Gary as he reads the letter and flips through the class catalog while he eats his cereal. This is it. It is official. He enjoys a peaceful breakfast while his mom is attending a teacher's workshop, and his dad is at work. Gary smiles to himself as he pictures the celebration his parents would insist upon. Tonight they will enjoy steaks at Clyde's in Brayton; there would be no arguing with his parents on that point.

Gary makes his decision of not announcing to anyone that he is officially leaving Reedville until after the tournaments are over. He knew he could contain the secret, but he doubts that his proud parents could duplicate the secrecy he desires. Whatever happens...happens. He shrugs at the thought.

He has to get to practice, but he indulges himself and looks through potential class selections. He spends a few more minutes flipping through the catalog, highlighting his core requirements, and dog-earing potential elective courses.

* * * * *

On the practice field the players are quiet as they warm up. They are lined up as usual, tossing the ball back and forth, as subdued as they have been all season, even after suffering the embarrassment of the opening round loss in the conference tourney. Coach Willis finally calls the team together, "Everyone gather 'round here!"

Coach Willis holds a sheet of paper as the team closes in around the coach in a tight semi-circle. The coach takes in the dour expressions of his team. "Who died?" he asks jokingly with a snort. "What's with the long faces?"

Coach Willis holds up the piece of paper in his hand. "You know what I got here?" He smiles, "Looks like we caught a break. You have a chance at redemption. We drew Clarkston in the first round. A rematch. Now you can make up for that flop of yours in the conference tournament."

There is a collective murmur of affirmation rumbling through the team. "Bootsy!" Coach Willis calls out.

Coach Booth approaches the team, "I have the schedule on a handout for everyone to take with them after hitting. Let's get some good rips in the cage today. Be sharp. Dave, you hit first. I'll throw to you."

The players spread out to their traditional positions in the field to shag balls as Coach Boots tosses to Dave. His season-long slump is no better in batting practice. Dave whiffs at batting practice speed pitches and the rare instance that he makes contact, he rolls dribblers down the first baseline.

"J-J-J-Jesus, Dave!" Tony yells from his usual position at deep short, almost left field. "Give us some action out h-h-h-here!"

Dave waves haplessly at a couple more pitches before stepping out of the box and adjusting his gloves. Tony shakes his head in disgust. "Thanks for the cool breeze, B-B-B-Big man!" he yells mockingly.

Dave heaves a sigh as he shakes his head beside himself with frustration. He finally makes contact and on back to back pitches. Minimal contact that dribbles the ball through the infield. The balls roll out to the dirt area that would be the normal shortstop position. Tony moves to the spot of the last two balls dribbled out to the field by Dave.

Gary trails behind him. Tony yells into Dave, "Here's the d-d-d-d-deal. I am going to stand h-h-h-h-here and give you a clean shot at my g-g-g-g-gonads." He throws down his glove and places his hands in a "v" shape pointing to his groin. "F-F-F-Free shot! All you have to do is h-h-h-hit a line drive, and you will c-c-c-c-cripple me for life!"

Tony kicks his glove away and shoves his hips forward, hands behind his back. Gary laughs and shakes his head as he stands next to Tony. "Come on, Dave," Gary yells, trying to provide some encouragement.

Tony cups his hands around his mouth, "Freeee sh-sh-sh-shot!" he hollers.

He drops his hands to his groin and cups himself, "F-F-F-Freeee shot!" he repeats before returning his hands to his hips.

Gary yells to Dave, "Hey, grab that new Easton with the green lettering that I've been using. It's a little lighter and brand-spanking new. I think you'll like it."

Dave exits the cage and grabs the new bat, taking a couple practice swings before stepping back to the plate. Coach Boots lays a fat pitch down the middle, and Dave smashes the ball on a line right at Tony. Dave is as surprised as anyone, but poor Tony is frozen in place about to pay the ultimate price for his mockery. At the last possible instant it is Gary to the rescue. He reaches to his glove side and snags the ball in front of Tony's groin. The momentum of the ball drives Gary's glove into Tony's crotch and buckles him. "No," Tony squeaks.

The blow Tony still suffers is painful, and he rolls around flopping in the dirt. A few tears squeeze from his eyes that he has pinched tightly closed and has yet to open.

Coach Boots pauses his pitching as the team in the field is falling down laughing at the suffering boy. Gary shakes his head as he stands over Tony. "I don't know why I did that. I could have let it go and prevented the world from being tortured by a plague of little Tonies."

Tony is flat on his back covering his balls with both hands as the pain subsides a bit. He lifts his head up and looks toward Dave sporting a wide grin. Dave points the bat at Tony in appreciation. "N-n-n-no need to thank me, D-D-D-Dave." Tony manages to gasp.

"Drag him off the field," Coach Boots commands and with the help of Fin and Gary, Tony is removed. He is dragged by his feet and his shirt rides up, exposing his big belly. He is dumped to the side of the batting cage like a beached whale, as batting practice resumes. Coach Boots fires more pitches to Dave who is suddenly tearing the cover off the ball, sending line drives all over the outfield. Tony lies sprawled in the grass on his back in the shade of the trees behind the batting cage. He stares at the sky and in between the clanks of the ball off the bat he yells, "Y-y-y-you are welcome, D-D-D-Dave!"

Everyone cycles through the batting cage in a long practice. When the final ball is rounded up, Coach Boots calls everyone to gather around in the shade of the giant cottonwood trees separating the ballpark from the parking lot. Coach Willis hangs back as Boots hands out the schedules of the Regional Tournament. "Guys, I have an announcement. I signed a thirty day contract to play minor league ball down in Iowa."

Boots takes a deep breath, "I hate to leave you hanging like this, but it is a dream come true for me to get a shot at baseball...and they pay me! I'm sorry about the timing. It couldn't be worse, but this could be my one and only chance." Boots looks around at the stunned faces surrounding him, "A chance of a lifetime," he adds trailing off.

"I knew it was true!" Lawrence shouts from the group. A murmur goes through the boys as Coach Boots' statement registers with them. Coach Boots raises his hands to quiet everyone, "I talked with Marv, er, I mean Coach Willis," he continues casting glances at the head coach. "My brother, Sammy, will take my place the rest of the year."

The team is stunned into stillness, absorbing the news. The silence is finally broken by clapping from one player. Gary claps his hands loudly and is quickly joined by the rest of the team, providing a round of applause for their coach. "Good luck, Coach," Dave shouts.

The applause diminishes as Coach Boots raises a hand in acknowledgement and to speak again. "Thanks, Dave. I have a request before I go. Hutton is hosting the state tourney this year. That is where I grew up." He enjoys his moment and looks around at all the faces listening to him. "So, nothing would give me more pleasure than to hear that you won the championship in my old home town."

A rousing cheer and applause goes up from the team. Gary steps forward and extends his hand for Coach Boots to shake. A line forms behind him, and each player offers a congratulatory and good luck handshake to their coach.

Chapter 30
The Road to Regions

    The regional tournament has arrived. The bus sits fully loaded at April's Café with notable exceptions; there is still no word from Chuck, and the team has concluded that his season is over. Another change is the man behind the wheel. Sammy Booth has replaced his brother and waits patiently for the signal from Coach Willis to get rolling. Sammy is a thinner, a rougher-around-the-edges, older copy of his brother Bobby. Sammy spent some time in the Air Force as an enlisted man before his discharge and return to South Dakota. Sammy had a special skill in the Air Force; he was part of a special unit that traveled the world representing Elmendorf Air Base in Anchorage, Alaska. Sammy was a gifted basketball player, and his job in the Air Force was just that, playing basketball. Technically, he was a fuels specialist, gassing up the planes that flew in and out of the air base, but that was just on paper. He was one of two white players on Elmendorf basketball team that circled the world throughout the year, playing against the other branches of the military in exhibitions and tournaments. For all practical purposes he was a professional basketball player. His uniform nine out ten days was the top-of-the-line silk sweat suit the team wore when traveling from base to base. The embroidered giant Kodiak bear head with mouth agape, teeth flashing menacingly on the warm-up jacket was the pride of Elmendorf, and the team represented the base well in competition.
    Sammy had enjoyed his time in the military, probably a lot more than most since all he had done was play basketball, but his time ran out. A knee injury on the court shortened his stint in the Air Force, and an honorable discharge with fifty percent disability bought him his ticket back to South Dakota. The Air Force had given Sammy a love for flying, and that's what he did now; he is a pilot for Ag Services Crop Spraying. He flew spray planes applying chemicals to farmers' fields, and he loves his job. He is thirty-two years old and fifty percent owner of the company. He is his own boss and when his brother asked him to take over coaching, it is a no brainer.

Sammy glances in the mirror at himself from his driver's seat. He smooths the jersey of his baseball uniform. He hasn't been in a sports uniform since he left the Air Force eight years ago. He catches Coach Willis' eye in the mirror as he asks the question, "Ready, Coach?"

Coach Willis sits in the first seat behind the driver. His arms are folded on his belly, and his eyes are half closed, "Yup, let's get 'er in gear."

Sammy nods and turns the key starting the bus. He swings the lever for the door, and it squeaks shut. Sammy has barely driven twenty feet, when from around the corner of the café, Chuck's pickup truck slides across the gravel parking lot in front of the bus. Sammy's pilot skills and quick reflexes allow him to slam on the brakes, throwing everyone on board for a lurch. "Holy shit!" Sammy yells. "What the fuck is this guy doing?"

Chuck's door on his pickup is already open, and the dust from his sliding stop clouds the view. Coach Willis has his eyes wide open after the bone jarring halt. "It's Chuck."

Chuck's mother emerges from the passenger side of the pickup, waving her hand in front of her face trying to clear the dust. Chuck has already thrown his gear on ground next to him as he waits for his mother to come around the truck. The whole team gathers to the side of the bus where all the action is to try to see what is going on.

Coach Willis limps down the steps. He turns to Sammy and gestures at the door. "Sorry," Sammy smiles sheepishly and flips the lever to open the door and let Coach Willis off the bus.

When the cloud of dust parts, Coach Willis finds himself peering down at a frowning, petite lady. "Hi, Miss Fisher," he greets her with a tip of his cap.

"Hello, Marvin. It's actually Mrs. Stevens now, but please call me Lorraine."

"Ok, Lorraine," Coach Willis nods.

"I had a little talk with Chuck's step-dad and found out that the tournaments are still going on," Lorraine remarks, putting her hands on her hips, clearly perturbed in recalling her conversation with her husband. "We've been busy with the early harvest, and well...when I found out that Mr. Stevens had prevented Chuck from playing ball...I about blew a gasket."

Lorraine reaches out and pulls her son to her side. "I'm sorry about this big commotion here in the parking lot," she sighs. "If it's not too late, I'd like to have Chuck join the team again. It wasn't his fault he missed the other games, so please don't hold that against him."

Coach Willis holds up a hand and waves away the apology. "No, no, Lorraine. No need to apologize at all. Just a bit of a communication issue sounds like to me. I see no problem. Step aboard, Chuck."

Chuck reaches down, grabs his gear, leans over, and kisses his mother's cheek before literally hopping on the bus.

On the bus Chuck is all smiles. He passes Sammy in the driver's seat, does a double take, and then walks backwards to Sammy, "You're new," Chuck drops his bag and extends his hand.

Sammy grasps Chuck's hand. "I'm the new Coach Boots. I am Sammy Booth, Bobby Jim's brother."

"Pleased to meet ya," Chuck nods and grips his gym bag, hoisting it over his head as he moves down the aisle of the bus.

"I'm back, baby!" Chuck yells a he trudges between the seats receiving high fives from all of his teammates.

Outside the bus Lorraine hugs Coach Willis. She breaks the hug but still grasps Coach's arms. "Thank you so much, Coach. If anything comes up you call and talk to me, not Mr. Stevens. Could you tell me all the game times for the tourney?"

"Well, we play at six o'clock tonight. If we win, we play tomorrow night at eight."

Lorraine nods and lets go of Coach Willis. "We'll be there."

Coach Willis tips his cap and steps back aboard the bus. He climbs the steps and places a hand on Sammy's shoulder. "Let's roll."

Chapter 31
Back on Track

Yorktown, South Dakota, is another town named after an East Coast village by the migrants moving west. It is a farm community in east central South Dakota. Yorktown is a redundant agricultural village with grain elevators and a water tower painted red, white, and blue along with a mammoth-sized Yorktown High School Mascot painted on its side, a Minute Man with the traditional tri-corner hat. Above and below the mascot the tower shouts in large lettering, "Yorktown Patriots."

Just about a hundred miles due south of Reedville, Yorktown has an additional economy of the railroad. The double tracks of the Burlington Northern Railroad pass through the town, and a rail maintenance workers' substation brings additional jobs to the bustling community. The tracks serves coal trains running lignite from the coal beds in Wyoming across South Dakota to power plants in the east.

Yorktown is an up and coming baseball program, and they have invested well in its facilities. It is a perfect stage for Reedville to shine. The rematch with Clarkston is a joke. The game is called by the 15-run rule after three innings, the final score is Reedville twenty four, Clarkston one. Trent pitches the three innings giving up only one hit, a home run that all players on both teams thought was the unlikeliest hit of the year. Even though Trent had pitched a nearly perfect game, he was razzed mercilessly by his teammates for giving up a home run to a pinch hitter in the bottom of the third inning. Clarkston's best player had broken his ankle, and he was getting his final at bat of his Teener career, cast and all. Trent did his best, but the one-legged batter tagged him for the lone blemish of the evening, awkwardly limping his way around the bases in a walking boot.

After the game it is back to the Yorktown Motor Inn where it is a quiet night for the team. Lights out at eleven o'clock; it is all business resting for the regional crown the next night.

In the region championship game it is more of the same. Yorktown as the host team provides little resistance to the dominating Reedville

Cardinals. Reedville hitters pound out hit after hit and make every play in the field flawlessly. In the fourth inning it is 15-1 in favor of Reedville as Chuck mows down hitters left and right. He has seven strikeouts out of the possible twelve outs through the fourth inning. With the game well in hand, Fin stands up from the dugout bench and stretches, "I'm going to the concession stand. Coach, you need anything?"

Sammy waves away the offer, "No, thanks."

Fin moseys his way to the concession stand carefree, knowing they are on the way to the state championship, but he is still hungry, and the celebration and trophy presentation might mean a long delay until his next meal. He stands in line studying the menu. He finally moves up to order. "Let me see...," he contemplates.

The clank of the metal bat rings out behind Fin. He is oblivious to the shuffling around him as he scratches his chin, "I will have...,"

He doesn't have a chance to finish his sentence, a foul ball curls over the protective netting and conks off Fin's head sending him to the ground. He drops from the sight of the concession stand worker, and she leans out to see what happened. "Are you okay?" she questions.

Fin gets to his knees; he swipes his hat from the ground angrily and feels the lump on top of his head. He looks at his fingertips and sees the sticky blood on his digits. He pushes himself to his feet whining and muttering, "Why is this always happening to me?"

The server looks wide-eyed at poor Fin and repeats, "Are you okay?"

Fin nods and presses on the knot on his head where the bean-ball-foul left its mark. He pulls his cap down on his head and looks at the server, "Could I have some ice," he points to his head, "for my head?"

The lady nods and as she turns away, Fin calls to her, "...and a hot dog...please?"

Snack in one hand, ice in the other, Fin heads back to the dugout. He is finishing the last bite of his hotdog as he goes down the final step of the dugout. Sammy looks up from the scorebook and does a double-take, seeing the bag of ice Fin is holding on his head. "What the hell happened to you?"

Coach Willis looks over from his perch on the bench to see what is going on. Fin lifts the bag of ice from his head and swallows part of the last bite of his hotdog. He speaks with his mouth full, mumbling, "I got hit on the head by a foul ball while in line at the concession stand."

Coach Willis shakes his head, "Of course you did," he states matter-of-factly.

The Coach turns his attention back to the game and sees the final weak ground ball sent to second base. Lawrence scoops it up and flips the ball to Tony at first, recording the final out of the game. The Reedville team gathers at the mound jumping up and down in celebration around the winning pitcher, Chuck. Fin gathers a lot of strange looks as the other players notice him, celebrating in the bouncing mass, one hand pressing down a bag of ice on his head. With the handshakes at home plate completed the public address system announces, "Congratulations Region Three Champs. Good luck at the State Tournament!"

Gary, Dave, Zach, and Fin room together at Yorktown Motor Inn. They are oblivious to the celebrating taking place in the other rooms. Kids wrestle on the beds and jump from bed to bed late into the night. The boys are exhausted by two in the morning, and the lights are finally out, but not before furniture is broken and beds are collapsed.

Everyone is asleep but one boy. In all the commotion of celebration, Chuck has slipped out for some fun of his own. At three-thirty in the morning a commotion in the parking lot brings a police car with lights flashing to the motel. The red and blue lights flash and reflect off the room windows. Curtains part as guests for the night at the Motor Inn look out their windows to see what is going on. Chuck is drunk and arguing with a police officer. Another police cruiser pulls into the lot.

"I didn't do anything!" Chuck shouts.

The taller of the two policemen barks orders. "Son, please put your hands on the car."

"I don't understand!" Chuck slurs and staggers.

"Put…your…hands…on…the…car!" the policeman repeats.

Chuck reluctantly complies and is handcuffed and searched.

"What did I do?" Chuck whines.

"For one thing," the officer begins, "it's three thirty in the morning and you are wandering the parking lot."

Chuck tries to shrug, struggling against his wrists clasped behind his back, "So?"

The officer shakes his head, "We received a disturbance call, and I pulled into see you kicking the devil out of the Coke machine."

Chuck is wobbly. He is incredulous, "What? It's illegal to get a Coke? The machine took my money, so I kicked it. Big deal."

Players are emerging from their rooms to witness the spectacle of Chuck. They are bleary-eyed as they look at their teammate. They shield their eyes from the flashing red and blue strobing lights.

The policeman puts his hand on Chuck's shoulder, "Have you been drinking, son? You reek of alcohol."

Chuck snorts a laugh, "No." He flatly denies the charge, followed quickly by, "Maybe a little."

The officer holds up a pint bottle of whiskey he has taken from an oversized pocket from Chuck's cargo shorts. Only a half-swallow of the amber fluid is left in the bottle. "Where did that come from?" Chuck questions mockingly. "That's not mine."

Coach Willis finally emerges from his room, joining the congregation in the parking lot. "What's going on officer? He's one of our players."

Chuck is loaded into the back of the police cruiser as the officer looks at Coach Willis. "This boy is under arrest for disorderly conduct, under age consumption, and public drunkenness. You can bail him out tomorrow."

The police cars pull out of the lot, leaving the team in stunned silence.

Chapter 32
Fallout

On the Tuesday following the Reedville Teeners' regional championship, all the players and their parents gather at April's Café. It isn't a briefing on the upcoming state tournament details; this is a meeting to address the aftermath of the debacle following the game in Yorktown. Everyone settles and Coach Willis pushes himself up from his seat at the bar and limps to the center of the room. "All right then," Coach Marvin Wills begins with his drawl. He holds up a piece of paper, "We have received a bill from the motel in Yorktown. As most of you know, there was some damage to many of the rooms. Broken chairs, beds, and whatnot."

Most of the parents nod ashamedly. Meanwhile players stare at the floor trying to avoid eye contact with any adult in the room. Coach Willis keeps turning to look at his entire audience. He is in the center of the room like a concert performer in the round, he spins in circles trying to address the entire group. "We divided the bill amongst the players…and coaches." Coach Willis emphasizes the coaches' part. "It comes to forty-eight dollars apiece."

The silence in the room is overwhelming. Finally a cough from a corner booth breaks the deafening quiet. Coach Willis continues, "The City already paid the bill, and we're just taking donations now to cover it. It seems fair, but this is strictly voluntary. No one will be forced to pay."

On that note Gary scoots out of his booth where he has been sitting with Dave. He moves across the room to where his parents sit at a table. Harry and Mary Hillmann sit with Dale and Cynthia, Dave's mom and dad. Gary's father sits stoically. He is a 40-year old version of Gary. With salt and pepper hair and round glasses, his professorial appearance would seem to be suited more to the university, but he has spent his entire career as an engineer with South Dakota Department of Transportation District Engineer's Office.

Across the table from Harry and Mary sit Dale and Cynthia; Dale is approaching three hundred pounds if he isn't there already. His job in the restaurant franchise business suits him. Jovial and non-threatening, he can sell whatever needs to be sold; he is a natural salesman. Cynthia is an odd partner for Dale. She was runner-up in the Miss South Dakota pageant twenty years ago. She was a knockout and not much had changed in twenty years, except that maybe she is now more attractive. The marriage was a reinforcement that looks weren't everything, especially if you had the sales skills of Dale. He would be the first to tell you the best work he ever did was selling himself to Cynthia.

With pained look and matching tone Gary presented his case to his parents, "This is ridiculous. My room didn't have damage; why should I pay?"

Gary searches his parents' faces. His head shakes and both hands point to his chest as his look questions the entire merit of this discussion. His father finally speaks, reaching a hand out to his son. "It's ok. I appreciate what you're saying, but this is a team. Go ahead, we'll handle this."

Gary is taken aback. "No," he simply replies and moves to the middle of the room next to Coach Willis.

"Gary, you have something to say?" Coach Willis steps aside.

"I do have something to say, Coach. Dave, Zach, Fin, and I had no damage to our room. I think people should take responsibility for what they do."

Gary frowns, "It is really disappointing to me that everyone is dragged down by a few people. That said...I believe that the people in my room should not be painted with the same brush that penalizes and punishes everyone for the crimes of a few."

Silence reigns and grips a stranglehold on the room as Gary walks over to the booth where Dave is sitting. The only sound is Gary's footsteps across the floor. Dave offers a fist bump of solidarity as Gary takes a seat. After a moment the first murmurs of contemplation regarding Gary's speech begin. After another minute the conversations break out in full force. Ten minutes pass, and Coach Willis has visited with every parent during this time. He moves back to the center of the room. "Can I have everyone's attention?"

He clears his throat, and the room quiets. "We have reached a consensus, and each player will be assessed forty-eight dollars for the room damage."

Gary is not surprised, but he can't contain his body language reflecting his disgust. He throws his hands in the air and shakes his head upon the announcement.

Coach Willis nods, satisfied with the agreement. "Thank you everyone. I'm now going to ask the parents to leave. The team has its own decision to make."

The parents shuffle out of the diner, surrounded by the tune of chairs scraping the floor and side conversations. The players on the team reconstitute in the back corner of the restaurant after just a few moments with the assurance that their meeting is parent-free. Standing as they listen to Coach Willis preach, they know what this executive session is about. Coach Willis has Sammy beside him. He purses his lips as he considers how to begin, "Fellas, you know the story."

He pauses as he stares over his players' heads searching for the words. "Ya know...I have always tried to let my teams police themselves."

Coach Willis turns to Sammy and puts his hand on his assistant coach's shoulder. "I debated over this quite awhile. I even consulted Sammy and picked his brain."

Sammy nods solemnly. Coach Willis removes his hand from the coach's shoulder and shrugs. "I finally decided I would indeed let you be the judge, jury, and if necessary...the hangman on this decision."

Coach Willis nods his head, satisfied with his comments. He heaves a heavy sigh and observes each face looking back at him. The grave expressions of the young men reflect the weight they carry on their shoulders with this decision. "Chuck," Coach Willis reaches a hand out toward the group, "come over here." Chuck moves front and center.

Coach Willis rests a hand on each shoulder of the boy standing before him. Chuck is nearly as tall as Coach. He maneuvers to the side of Chuck and continues to address the team, still resting his hands on the young man's shoulders. "Everyone knows what happened at the motel. We found out today there are no formal charges pending against Chuck. The police never read him his rights, and everything was dropped. That doesn't mean nothing happened. We all saw it. And now...we stand here listening. Chuck, do you have anything to say?"

Coach Willis releases his grip on the boy. Chuck looks at his peers. His eyes water, and he rubs at them trying to compose himself. He is a little shaky, but steadies himself. He stammers as he tries to speak, "I-I-I-I'm sorry."

Chuck breaks the ice with his apology and relaxes a bit. "I don't know what else I can say. I made a mistake."

He shrugs and surveys the faces staring at him. "I know I embarrassed everyone, and I'm really sorry."

Chuck scratches at his ear. He has never been more sincere. He cocks his head, "I completely understand if you don't want me on the team anymore. I accept full responsibility for my actions. It was stupid...a stupid mistake by a stupid kid."

No one reacts. The silence in the room is oppressive. Chuck makes one final plea, "I really want to stay on the team."

Chuck throws his hands in the air and shrugs, "I ask for your forgiveness...an' I promise you this...it will never happen again."

Coach Willis steps forward and places a hand on Chuck's shoulder, directing him to the exit. "I'm going to have Chuck step outside with me and Sammy. You guys can talk about it. I ask that you take a vote and come and get us to let us know your decision."

Coach Willis nods to Sammy and starts to lead Chuck away but is halted by a voice. "Chuck," Gary calls out.

Chuck turns along with the two coaches and faces Gary. "Just so you know, I'm voting to kick you off the team."

Chuck acknowledges Gary's comment with a slight nod. He drops his head and marches out in front of the two coaches as a man being lead to the gallows.

Chuck and the coaches disappear outside. Coach Willis's comments alluding to judge and jury go well with the courtroom-like debate the players have. "Anyone have anything to say?" Gary picks up where he left off. "I think I've made it clear where I stand. I will be embarrassed to play in the state tournament with him on my team."

Gary gestures over his shoulder with his thumb in the direction of Chuck's departure. "I like to win as much as the next guy. Heck maybe even more than the next guy...but I know what's gone on. It's in the papers; lots of people know what happened. We'll be the laughingstock of the tourney with people thinking we'll do anything to win...nope, that's not for me."

Gary searches his fellow players' faces. Most stare at the floor. "You guys vote the way you want, but I've said my piece."

Jesse and Turner lead a faction of the team that is best friends with Chuck, and they rise to his defense. First with Jesse. "C'mon. He said he was sorry."

Turner echoes the comment. "He promised it would never happen again."

Surprisingly Aric's comments carried the most weight. He stepped out in front of the group, foregoing his usual self-consciousness, and he spoke well and from the heart. "Guys, he did something stupid. There is no denying that fact." Aric nods in agreement with his own statement, "But if doing something stupid was a crime, I'd probably be serving life in jail."

A ripple of laughter flows through the team, drawing a smile even from Gary.

Zach holds up his cast. "Hear, hear," he chimes in.

"Yeah, you see?" Aric points to Zach. "Has anyone forgot about me nearly killing Zach when I backed over him?"

Aric doesn't wait for an answer, "How stupid was I for doing that? We all do stupid things." Aric looks away from his teammates at the wall for a moment, gathering his closing argument. "He stays on the team as far as I'm concerned."

"Let's go ahead and vote then," Gary steps forward. "Majority rules, raise your hand and say 'aye' if you want Chuck to stay on the team."

There is a chorus of "ayes" and hands raised as most of the players vote to keep Chuck on the team.

"Those against, raise your hand," Gary conducts the vote as he raises his own hand.

Dave, Zach, and Fin raise their hands joining Gary to expel Chuck from the team. "He stays on the team," Gary announces disgustedly. "I'll go let them know."

Gary spins away from the group. "See ya, Dave. I gotta get outta here."

Gary storms out of the café door and passes Chuck and the coaches in the parking lot. Without looking up Gary informs the group, "He stays on the team."

Gary stomps toward his truck in the crowded parking lot. Behind him Chuck pumps his fist. He shakes hands with Sammy and Coach Willis.

Chapter 33
Truce

When Gary exits the café in a huff, he has no idea he is followed. Annie trails after Gary. She is waiting tables and witnesses the debates from the opposite side of the room. She knows it is a contentious issue. She passes by her Uncle Marvin and tosses her apron to him as she goes by. "See you later," she whispers in passing to her uncle.

Gary reaches his truck and yanks open the door, but is halted before climbing into the vehicle with a soft spoken voice of concern. "Aren't you going to say, 'hi'?" Annie questions from a distance.

Gary turns and sees Annie standing in the fading light of evening, her hands clasped at her waist. "Sorry. Hi, Annie," Gary manages a weak smile.

"Are you okay?" Annie questions further. "I know the meeting tonight was pretty brutal."

"I'm fine," Gary shrugs leaning on his door as it sways, not finding the catch to hold the door half-open. "I just needed to get out of there." He nods at the building.

Annie moves a couple steps toward Gary closing the distance to about ten feet. "I miss you. I thought about it a lot. I'm sorry. I had all these great expectations, and I...I am sorry."

"You don't have to apologize. I should have told you right away. But, I didn't. I wasn't even accepted yet. But, hey, I just got the final notice the other day. I made it."

"Congratulations!" Annie exclaims. "I really mean it."

"Thanks," Gary smiles and nods. "It's a big deal to me."

Annie moves closer to Gary and extends her arms. "How about a congratulatory hug?"

"Sure."

Annie steps forward, and Gary hugs her. A few players emerge from the café, and Gary hears their voices and looks up. He breaks the hug off quickly. "I'm sorry. I gotta get away from here. I can't be around these guys right now."

Gary moves to climb in the truck. "Can I come with you?" Annie questions.

"Don't you have to work?"

"I'll just ditch. Uncle Marv can close down tonight."

Gary gives a nod, and Annie runs around the truck and leaps into the passenger side. Gary steers the truck out of town as darkness settles and the streetlights flicker on. The pair drives out to the country, away from the lights of town. Annie slowly scoots herself across the bench seat and soon finds her head resting on Gary's shoulder. Gary finds an approach to a cornfield off the gravel road and pulls up to the edge of the corn, killing the engine and the headlights in the secluded spot.

* * * * *

The doors of the truck open and darkness is sliced by the cab light. Quickly, the doors are shut and the only light is the last pale hue to the west as stars emerge in full display on the cloudless night. "C'mon," Gary pleads. "We'll just lay down in the back of the truck and watch the stars come out…just for a little while."

"I don't know," Annie balks.

It had taken some convincing for Annie to even get out of the truck, but here she is stepping up on the back bumper, swinging her leg over the tailgate, and stepping up into the truck bed. Gary follows carrying a couple sweatshirts to spread out in the dusty bed of his truck, his duffle bag for a pillow. Annie's attention is skyward and distracting stars overhead cause her to stagger. "Watch it!" Gary warns, dropping the gear and catching her before she stumbles right out of the truck. "You all right?" Gary questions.

"That's embarrassing," Annie mumbles, pulling away from Gary.

"Move, and I'll spread these jackets so we can lie down." Gary repositions Annie with a tug of her arm.

He spreads the coats on the truck bed. He reaches into his duffle bag and removes something and quickly puts it in his pocket before tossing the duffle into position. Lying down on his back and staring up at the sky, he pats the spot next to him. "View is pretty good from here."

Annie doesn't say anything about what he took out of the bag. Instead she kneels down reluctantly and finally lays on her back, snuggling close to Gary and sharing the duffle bag as a pillow. They each fold their hands on their chest and stare at the sky. The dog days of the last week of July have been given a temporary reprieve from the standard summer oppressive heat and humidity. A cool north breeze rustles the leaves on the corn. Gary notes the wind. "You are witnessing and enjoying a miracle."

"Really?" Annie inquires.

"Yeah. Ninety-nine out of a hundred days we couldn't do this. We'd be eaten alive by mosquitoes."

"Well, isn't that special?" Annie replies with her best Saturday Night Live Church Lady impression.

Gary laughs, but is interrupted by a falling star streaking across the sky for several seconds. "Wow!" Annie yells. "Did you see that?"

"Yeah. Beautiful."

The words are tricky for Annie. She turns her head trying to view Gary in the dark and attempting to understand Gary's meaning. She decides not to read into the comment and returns her gaze skyward. "I've never seen anything like that before. That was awesome," she whispers. "You just don't get this view in the Cities with all the lights."

She feels for Gary's hand and grasps it. Gary does not resist. They lie on their backs in silence staring at the stars, searching the constellations and hoping for another meteor to flash into the atmosphere.

Minutes pass with only the sound of crickets and the gusts of wind shuffling through the corn. Gary turns to his side to try to see Annie. His eyes have adjusted to the darkness, and he can make out the slightest silhouette. Annie turns her head to meet his eyes. She refuses to make solid eye contact and her eyes twitch back and forth between Gary and the stars above. "I have something for you," Gary whispers.

Annie giggles. "I know," she whispers back. "I can feel it against my leg."

"What?" Gary cries out, "No! Get your mind out of the gutter. I'm trying to be serious."

Annie laughs. "Gol-leeee. I'm just kidding. Take it easy."

Gary props himself up on his elbow and reaches into his oversized shorts pocket.

Annie shakes her head as she watches Gary dig in his pocket. "So help me God, if you pull your hand out of your pocket with your middle finger raised and flip me off, I will give you a fat lip."

Gary laughs, "What is with you?"

"I don't know if I'm ready," Annie mumbles meekly, her eyes are focused on Gary's pocket a moment before turning up to meet his eyes.

Gary is puzzled, "Ready for what?"

"Are you getting a condom out of your pocket? I saw you take something from your duffle bag."

Gary laughs and his head falls back to the duffle bag pillow as he takes his hand from his pocket pulling a chain with a medallion dangling from the end. He holds the chain up high at arm's length, and it dangles over Annie's head as she reaches a hand toward it in the starlight. "What is it?" she whispers.

"I hope you are not too disappointed. It's not a condom," Gary replies dejectedly.

"I can see that," Annie snaps, snatching the chain out of the air and pulling it close to her eyes.

Gary lets go of the medallion and chain. "It's my Saint Christopher's medal."

Annie nods in realization, and Gary watches her in silence for a moment as she turns the medal over in her hands feeling the coolness of the metallic material. Gary continues, "My grandpa gave it to me. Saint Christopher is the patron saint for travelers, and it's supposed to be for good luck."

"You want me to have it?" Annie questions.

"Sure."

"I can't take this," she pushes the medal back to Gary.

"I want you to have it." Gary curls his hand over the top of Annie's, imbedding the medal into her palm. "I want you to remember this summer…always."

Gary extracts the medal from her hand and sits up. He places the chain over Annie's head as she leans up to accept the necklace. "There. It's yours. You'll hurt my feelings if you don't take it."

Annie returns Gary's smile. "I know it's kind of gaudy, but you don't have to wear it," Gary shrugs. "I just kept it in my bag with my baseball stuff. I'd get it out, rub it for luck, and think about my grandpa before each game."

Gary lies on his back and looks back to the stars. Annie does the same. She holds the medallion in her hand and traces the edge with her fingers as she stares at the stars.

"My grandpa was a war hero. He died a couple years ago. He never got to see me play Teeners and win a championship," Gary speaks softly in a monotone. "All I remember about him is how awesome he was as a grandfather. He knew everyone, and everyone seemed to know him…and they liked him."

Annie turns to Gary. She pushes herself up and kisses him on the mouth. "Thanks," she whispers barely audible to Gary's ears.

"I know we have different journeys ahead of us," she speaks clearly now as she falls to her back snuggling close to Gary again. "I shouldn't have gotten angry with you and wasted time in pettiness."

Annie's hair twitches as she shakes her head, disappointed with herself. Her voice gets higher as she continues, "I was just enjoying things so much. I didn't want it to end….ever. When that envelope hit the counter, and I heard what your mom said, then I saw the seal of prep school…that just broke the spell. I just lost it."

Gary grimaces and nods, "I hear ya. I guess that's why I didn't say anything either. I didn't want the spell to be broken."

With the dexterity of a feline, Annie spins from her position on her back. She straddles Gary on her knees. "What are you doing?" Gary whispers hoarsely in surprise.

Annie pulls her shirt over head and tosses it aside as she reaches behind her back and undoes her bra, revealing her milky white breasts in the starlight, starkly contrasting the rest of her tan torso. She flicks her bra towards her shirt. Grabbing Gary's hands, she places them on her chest. The Saint Christopher medallion raps at Gary's knuckles as he feels her nipples in the palms of his hand. "I don't know if this is a good idea…" Gary's voice trails off as he looks skyward. Annie leans forward and kisses Gary's mouth. "Shhh," she cajoles softly. "You gave me something, now I have something for you."

"Annie…" Gary protests with a whisper.

"Shhh," is her only response as she unbuttons his cargo shorts, feeling the bulge straining the buttons.

"Tonight's your lucky night," Annie whispers.

She adjusts her weight on her hands as she straddles Gary. She leans forward to kiss him again, and the medallion around her neck cracks across the bridge of Gary's nose, and he muffles a cry, "Ahhh,"

"Sorry," Annie giggles.

Annie climbs to the side of Gary. She reaches for his exposed erection. In her hand the member is warm. She slowly strokes up and down, straining her eyes in the dim light, curiously observing for a moment or two, the first male organ she has ever touched. Finally, she turns back to see Gary's face. She reflects his smile as Gary relaxes, accepting the gift. His hands move behind his head. His eyes look up. He stares to the sky, noting a jet passing miles overhead. Its lights flash and the contrail is visible even in the starlight.

Chapter 34
Coach Sammy

The sun is shining down on another summer day. The morning practice is about to commence, but, before batting practice starts, the coaches gather the team. The antsy players finally settle down, encircling Sammy and Coach Willis. "Settle down, fellas," Coach Willis pleads. "Sooner we get done with some of these here announcements, the sooner we can hit." Coach Willis smiles at his players; he can see the energy and desire to win finally taking hold. "Coach Sammy has some details on the state tournament. Take it away, Sam."

Coach Sammy Booth takes a deep breath. He is feeling the energy and the competitive spirit for the first time in a long time. His knee hurts, and he shuffles in place, trying to get comfortable on his bowed legs. He is nervous for reasons that he has no fathomable idea about, just the thrill of competition he reckons. "Listen up now. You probably are aware the state tourney is in Hutton. Hutton has only one motel, and it's already full. The team will be staying in Yankton. It's only about ten miles away."

Tony interrupts in his usual manner, "Where the hell is Hutton?"

"Near Yankton," Sammy responds. "I.e., we are staying in Yankton."

Fin raises his hand. Sammy nods granting the question. Fin's puzzled look indicates his confusion, "Is Yankton near Rapid City?"

"What?" Sammy's voice rises. "No! Don't you know anything about South Dakota geography?"

Tony shrugs, "I think it's p-p-p-pretty obvious we don't."

"What are they teaching you in school?" Sammy's voice goes even higher. He continues, "Well...never mind. Just tell your parents the team will be staying in Yankton." Sammy takes another deep breath, "More importantly..."

Coach Sammy cuts himself off. He looks over the players staring back at him. He reaches down and rubs his aching knees before catching Coach Willis' eye. The Coach gives Sammy a nod, encouraging him to proceed. The coaches had spoken about a pep talk for the team after the difficult meeting the night before. It was decided it was a good idea that Sammy deliver the speech. Coach Sammy heaves another deep breath as the players eye him suspiciously. He takes his cap off and sweeps the beads of sweat forming on his brow back across his hair as he smooths his unkempt locks, finally pulling his cap down firmly on his head, he straightens the bill perfectly.

"We have an opportunity," Sammy finally begins.

He catches Coach Willis out of the corner of his eye. The Coach nods approvingly in agreement.

"Here's the way I see it, boys...men. I looked at the tournament schedule. As you know this is a single elimination tournament. One loss, and you're out of the run for the championship. There's no 'do over'. Basically, we are far and away the favorite."

Coach Sammy pushes back from the group a bit and begins to pace. Dave and Gary catch each other's eye and shrug as they watch and listen to their coach.

"We can win this thing; no, we are going to win this thing. It's going to take concentration." Sammy stops and feels the questioning eyes boring through him. "So, let's start today with this batting practice. That's the theme, concentration. Eye on ball. Know your job. Concentration."

Sammy extends his hand, "Everybody, put your hand in on top of mine; concentration on three. One, two..."

The team crushes forward and piles their hands on top of Sammy's. When Sammy says, "Three," the team pushes the pile of hands up in the air and shouts, "Concentration!" The cheer is a less than simultaneous chant with a few late stragglers repeating the word.

Nonetheless, Sammy is pumped up by his own motivational speech. He shouts out the order, and players start to disperse. His full competitive-sports mode is kicking in. "All right! I'll throw to the first four batters. Let's get somebody in the cage! Hustle!"

The team's enthusiasm is not quite what Sammy had envisioned and as the players move to their usual positions to shag balls, Coach Willis walks with Sammy to the pitchers mound. The men limp together in step. "Don't worry," Coach Willis comforts. "They'll warm up to ya."

Coach Willis slaps Sammy on the shoulder and walks behind the batting cage to observe the hitters.

* * * * *

As batting practice commences, Dave, Gary, Tony, Fin, and Lawrence cluster together in their usual spot, short left field, just beyond where the shortstop would play. The steady clank of metal bat on ball rings out. The boys field a periodic line drive or grounder. It is pretty low key. Dave eyeballs Gary and notices that he is smiling. He finally calls him out, "What are you so smiley about today? You've barely said two words. I thought you'd be pretty grumpy after the meeting last night."

Gary's smile widens. Fin fields a grounder next to Dave and tosses the ball to Jesse, shagging balls at the mound for Sammy. "I know why he's smiling," Fin smirks. "He was with Annie. I saw her get into his truck after the meeting."

"Wow," Dave bounces his eyebrows. "Good for you."

Gary holds up his hand, "I smile because I had a premonition of victory last night. That's all I got to say."

Dave winces, "What the hell does that mean? You and Annie...spill it."

Gary shakes his head, "A gentleman does not kiss and tell." Gary smiles and shrugs. "Not to change the subject drastically, but I will anyway. Is it just me, or is Sammy weirder than Boots?"

Tony is leaning on his bat as he stands in the outfield. He'd rather work on his offensive skills than bother with fielding batting practice grounders. He throws down his glove, raises the bat, and takes a few practices swings. "Yeah, what the hell was that all about earlier? His big rah-rah speech and inspirational 'hands-in' cheer?"

Tony sticks out his hand and throws it up in the air and yells mockingly, "C-c-c-concentrate!"

Tony puts a donut-shape weight on the bat and takes a couple more swings as he watches Sammy throw and times his swing with the batting practice pitch. "We've never done this motivational stuff before."

Dave fields a hot ground ball very slickly on his backhand and nonchalantly tosses it in to Jesse. The others admire his fielding skill silently with a nod. Dave shakes his head as he considers the conversation about Sammy, "He's a motivator. Man, he seems to take this stuff seriously. I hope he doesn't stroke out on us."

Lawrence pipes up, "My dad said he was pro-level point guard. He was in the Air Force, and his job was to play basketball."

Tony sneers at Lawrence, "What are you? The B-B-B-Booth family historian?"

Lawrence shrugs, "I'm just telling you what I heard. My point is that he is ultra-competitive."

Tony stops his practice swings, inverts the bat, and slams the bat down to remove the donut-shaped weight from his bat. He stoops and picks up the weight and eyes it. "D-D-D-D-did you guys hear about that guy that got his d-d-d-dick stuck in a barbell weight?"

"What are you talking about?" Dave mocks.

"I heard it on the news, P-P-P-Paul Harvey or something," Tony continues. "He stuck his dick in the hole of the w-w-w-w-weight where the b-b-b-b-bar would go. H-H-H-His cock swelled up, and they had to do surgery to d-d-d-d-rain the blood or something. N-N-N-National news!"

Everyone groans and winces as each boy grabs at his own crotch in discomfort at just hearing about the incident. They stand silent for a few moments as they think about it. Finally Tony speaks up again, "That kinda h-h-h-happened to me once."

"What?" Gary sneers. "You got your dick stuck in a weight lifter? What was his name?"

Dave high fives Gary, and everyone laughs. Even Tony can't help but laugh at the slam he has endured. The butt of the joke, Tony's laugh fades quickly and he pouts.

Gary frowns, "Ohhh, I'm sorry. Go ahead. Finish telling your dick story."

Tony perks back up. He excitedly recounts the story, "Anyway, my mom was b-b-b-babysitting this little kid. And the kid had one of those little p-p-p-pyramid type toys with rings of different colors of increasing s-s-s-s-size."

"Yeah, I've seen 'em," Dave nods. "Oh, no," He shakes his head. "Don't tell me…"

Tony continues his story, "I t-t-t-took that toy to the b-b-b-b-bathroom with me, and, well…let's just say one of those rings was d-d-d-d-destroyed. Thank God they were p-p-p-p-plastic and…"

Gary interrupts, "Enough! We get the picture."

Batting practice continues, and everyone gets their swings in. When practice wraps up for the day, Sammy calls everyone around, "Practice same time tomorrow morning. Get your hands in here."

Hands pile in on top of Sammy's, "Teamwork on three. One, two…"

On the count of three, everyone is with one voice and the yell goes out, "Teamwork!"

Chapter 35
Devastation

Gary is home alone enjoying his breakfast cereal before the last Reedville Teener practice of the year. It is on to the state tourney tomorrow, and they might take batting practice in Hutton, but this is it for Gary as far as real practice would go. The finale of his Teener career is in the back of his mind, and the thought doesn't bother him. He reads the paper and keeps an eye on the clock, still twenty minutes before he has to go. A knock on the front door interrupts his reading about the Minnesota Twins victory the night before. Gary opens the door and finds Annie sobbing and out of breath. She throws herself at Gary, and he catchers her in self defense. "Oh, my God!" Gary calls out as he wraps his arms around the inconsolable girl. "What's wrong?"

Between gasps and sobs, Annie wails, "He's dead! He's dead!"

"What, I don't...I can't understand you," Gary soothes as he tries to hold Annie upright. She sways and is collapsing as the sobs heave through her body.

Gary thinks he hears the words, "He's dead," but the phrase has no context.

Gary holds Annie tight and strokes her hair. He rocks her back and forth in his arms as one would soothe a baby. After a minute or two Annie regains her breath, "Uncle Marvin...he's dead."

"Oh, my God," Gary responds in a whisper.

He grips Annie as tightly as he dares and continues to rock her. She is finally able to speak more than two words at a time, and the words flow like an auctioneer, in fits and bursts. "He just never woke up this morning. April had to go to Brayton for an early eye appointment. And when Uncle Marv didn't show up at the café, I ran home to check...and...and..."

The sobs rip through her again, and Gary tries to ameliorate the shudders raging through her body. Annie pulls back from Gary to wipe her eyes. "He was still in bed...I touched him to wake him...he didn't move. I put my hand on his cheek....he was cold."

Gary pulls Annie back into his arms. He kisses the top of her head. He has tears in his eyes seeing her devastation. "God…I'm so sorry. What can I do?"

Gary stands holding Annie in his arms in the hallway next to the front door for minutes. It is Annie that pushes the door open and pulls Gary outside. "Please, just walk me home."

Gary nods. They move to the sidewalk along the street. Four blocks away they can see the emergency lights flashing outside the Willis household. The police chief's cruiser and an ambulance block the street. They walk slowly, silently. A block passes before Annie speaks. "I called 911 and ran out as fast as I could. To you. Like a frightened little girl."

Gary stops Annie in her tracks and wraps his arms around her. "It's ok. I'm here. Whatever you need. Tell April I'm here. My family is here. Anything you need."

* * * * *

Word is out and the Teener players convene to the baseball field and sit in the bleachers. An hour passes and the last straggling player shows up at the field. There is no coach or equipment, and the team sits in the bleachers quietly waiting, wondering what to do.

The shock of Coach Willis' death has subdued the usual joking and jostling in the energetic teenage boys. It is the first cognizant brush with death for many of the boys; Coach is a father figure to these guys. Sure, these individuals had been subjected to a grandparent dying, but for the vast majority of the team, death is something that happened to others and other families. The team is like a family, and they are now going through this…this void, this emptiness, and gut wrenching emotion together, a shared, yet, unwanted experience.

Time drags. Gary finally speaks, breaking the crushing silence. He talks to no one in particular. "Has anyone ever noticed your parents turn to the obituaries as the first thing they read in the paper?"

There is no response from anyone, and he continues. "I guess this is one of those things that," Gary stops to make quotation marks with his fingers, "I'm just too young to understand."

Chuck sits as far as he can from Gary and still be on the bleachers. The relationship between Gary and Chuck is probably something that will never get to a point of friendship. They just carefully keep their distance from each other. Teammates only, they'll never be buddies, and each is ok with that. They each had their own clique of friends on the team.

There is no necessity for deep bonds between everyone. From his position kitty-corner at the top of the bleachers from Gary, Chuck speaks, "I can't believe this. First Bootsy takes off; now Coach Willis is gone."

Heads nod and Chuck continues, "Here we are, stuck with Sammy as coach."

"Shhh," Aric cautions. "Sammy's coming."

Sammy Booth walks, head down, shoulders slumped, from the parking lot to the baseball field. He stands before the team and apologizes, "Sorry I am late. I realize nobody wants to be here."

He scans the pale, long faces in the bleachers before him. Sammy doesn't know what to say to these young men. It is a bad dream, and he can't wake from it. He purses his lips, "I do have some announcements. Aric's dad volunteered and will help coach at the state tourney."

He nods as if he could feel the question in everyone's' minds, "Yes, we are still going. There is no question that Coach Willis would have wanted us to compete."

Coach Sammy paces in front of the team. It is his team now and he is bound and determined to do what he can for these boys. It is what everyone needs to hear, a bit of normalcy that could distract them for the moment. Everything Sammy says is done matter-of-factly. "I will need everyone's jerseys. We are going to have black arm bands and patches with Coach's initials sewn on them."

The players nod at the idea, and Sammy continues with his list of discussion points as he paces back and forth. "Also, I did talk to April just before I came here. The funeral will not be until next week, after the tournament."

Sammy halts his pacing and stands before the team. He debates whether to say anything more. He fights his own emotions. His lip trembles imperceptibly, he can feel his own pain in his watery eyes. "One more thing," his voice cracks. "Coach Willis was a great coach, but more than that, he was a great man. I'm sure you don't know this, but he was my coach almost twenty years ago. He taught everyone how to get the most out of their talents on the field."

Sammy smiles, "The funny thing is that I didn't even realize it was more than baseball. He taught me how to make the most of whatever I was doing, on or off the field. It was a lesson I didn't even know I had learned until years later."

Sammy pauses. He nods, affirming his own words, "He was a good man, a good leader, and a role model. Years from now, just like me, you are going to look back at your baseball days and say 'Wow, I learned a lot.' Believe me, it'll happen, and you'll be glad you played baseball."

Sammy scans his players' faces. He is relaxed and confident. "I'm glad I can be your coach. That's it."

The players stand, but Sammy calls out, "Hey, one more thing. If anyone wants to hang around and take some hitting you are welcome to stay. Just remember, the bus leaves at 9:00 am tomorrow. Now...that's it." Sammy manages a half smile.

Sammy's speech hits home to the players, endearing him to these boys forever. Everyone stays, and Sammy throws the entire batting practice session. It is back to business as usual, at least in the baseball world of the Reedville Teeners.

Chapter 36
Tourney Road

The bus is loaded and ready to roll at nine o'clock sharp. They are underway, down the road, all present and accounted for. Coach Sammy is in charge, alone with the team still in a subdued mood. Aric's dad has volunteered to help coach, but he is traveling down separately. He is going to chauffer his wife and other kids the 250 mile trip from the north part of the state down to the southern border of South Dakota. Lawrence, also known as the Music Master for his wide ranging musical preferences, has some classic rock music on his custom recorded cassette tape. It is heavily laden with Credence Clearwater Revival. Good old CCR is what Lawrence thought of as appropriate an salve for their wounds... grieving music: "Have You Ever Seen the Rain," "Who'll Stop the Rain," "Lodi," and "Run Through the Jungle" intermingled with the more upbeat "Hey Tonight," "Bad Moon Rising," and "Fortunate Son" provide a reflective mood with enough energy to prepare for the games ahead, starting tonight.

The team divides up into its usual groups for playing cards. Today it's just Spades, and Gary and Dave as partners are smashing their opponents, Tony and Fin at this particular moment. The conversation is sparse, and competition is a little heated. In the first hour, threats of new card partnerships are uttered first softly then more vehemently.

The bus begins to slow, and it catches the attention of Dave immediately, "What's going on? Why we stopping in Summit? We've been on the road less than an hour?"

Sammy gets up from the driver's seat, "I just gotta pick something up," he calls back to the team before bolting off the bus.

"He's just gotta piss," Tony mumbles. "You know how old people get. Just play your cards."

The Quick Stop gas station just off Interstate 29 is a bustling place. Sammy is off the bus and back on carrying an Army duffle bag and a suitcase in less than a minute. He has the whole attention of the team as he stashes the bags on a seat near the front of the bus. "What's with the luggage? Did we get some new equipment?" Dave asks from the back of the bus.

Lawrence quickly chimes in, "New, lucky bats, perchance?"

Everyone's attention is focused on Sammy stowing the gear in a seat. "Come on, Sammy," Chuck exhorts. "What's up?"

Sammy doesn't acknowledge the questions; he just secures the new cargo. The thumping of feet stomping up the two steps of the bus entryway solves the mystery of the inexplicable stop. The team shares a collective gasp at the appearance of the man getting on the bus. "Coach Boots?" Chuck shouts the question on each player's mind. "What are you doing here?"

Bobby Booth produces a child-like wave, acknowledging everyone, "Hey, guys. The team is playing in St. Paul, and I asked for a couple days off. I thought I might help coach."

Coach Boots waves his other hand, flashing a burdensome cast on his arm just up to and short of his elbow. "I also took a foul ball off my arm and broke a bone in my wrist. The team told me to just go on home…so, I'm here to help!"

A cheer goes up from the team, welcoming their old coach back to the fold. Coach Boots smiles and sits in the driver's seat. He fires up the bus, and they pull back onto the Interstate headed south.

Chapter 37
Pit Stop

Three hours into the state tourney road trip and it was noon. The growling of stomachs and grinding of gears brought the team bus to the home of "hot eats and cool treats" the travelers stop sign indicated by white letters of DQ on a red background. The Dairy Queen is a South Dakota staple for fast food joints, and the team and coaches overwhelmed the counter of the Dairy Queen. Tony, Fin, Gary, and Dave stand at the counter and contemplate the menu above them. Fin is the first to decide on his lunch preference. He orders the daily special and grabs his wallet from his cargo shorts to extract payment. Tony scrunches his face, puzzled by the wallet in Fin's hand, "Wh-Wh-What is that?" he stutters and points.

Fin holds it up, "It's just my billfold."

Tony's bewilderment continues, "I-I-I-Is that Kenny Roger's f-f-f-face on your billfold?"

Gary and Dave turn their attention to the conversation between Fin and Tony. They eye Fin's wallet and smile, both eager to comment.

"Yeah, it's Kenny Rogers. What about it? My mom gave it to me!" Fin retorts defensively.

Gary grabs Fin's arm and turns the hand holding the wallet to get a better view. Gary laughs the words, "Kenny Rogers!"

Dave frowns, "Seriously, Fin? What are you, six years old?"

Fin shakes his head and shrugs, "What? It works perfectly fine as my wallet."

Tony, Dave, and Gary laugh and roll their eyes. "Just pay the lady," Dave urges as he pushes Fin all the way up against the counter.

Fin unbuttons the snap holding the two imitation leather halves of the billfold together, takes out his money and pays for his meal. The rest follow with their orders. The team relaxes in the restaurant, and everyone enjoys their variety of ice cream dessert, some indulging more than others.

Coach Boots gives the order for the team to get back on the bus, and Fin and a couple other players decide they want a small cone to enjoy on the road. Fin is one of the last to climb aboard the bus, and he is met with

Gary, Tony, and Dave lying in wait. The trio breaks out singing the classic Kenny Roger's ballad, "The Gambler."

Gary sings by himself, "You got to know when to hold 'em."

He is backed up with Tony and Dave, echoing the last words of each line, "When to hold 'em!"

Gary continues, "Know when to fold 'em."

Tony and Dave shriek, "When to fold 'em!"

Tony and Dave run in place as Gary finishes his last line, "Know when to walk away, and know when to run."

The bus reverberates with laughter at poor Fin's expense, but it rolls off his back as he shrugs and smiles, licking his ice cream cone. Gary puts his arm around Fin's shoulder. "You know, Fin, you are a good sport, and from this day forward, you will be known as 'The Gambler.'"

Gary shakes Fin's hand, bestowing the nickname.

Dave interjects, waving a finger of warning, "That's not a hard and fast rule. We may also refer to you as 'Kenny,' 'Roger,' 'Roge,' or 'Maharaja.' We expect you to respond appropriately."

Players laugh uncontrollably, falling across the seats, holding their sides, and wiping tears from their eyes.

Gary lets Fin proceed to his seat on the bus and calls out to the backseat, "Hey, Lawrence, what do you say? Can we get some country music on the stereo in honor of our special guest, Mr. Kenny Rogers?"

Lawrence flips the boombox to the FM radio input and tunes through static until he comes across the Nitty Gritty Dirt Band belting out their hit "Fishin' in the Dark."

The team sings along to the simple tune, relaxing and returning to form, slowly putting distance between themselves and the painful news of the week. The comic relief helps push the sorrow from their minds.

The country music portion of the road trip comes to a halt, and, with Lawrence at the controls of the boombox, he cuts off the country twang and blasts Eazy-E's "Eazy-Duz-It" as the bus rolls down the highway.

At the front of the bus Coach Boots steers the vehicle down the road and Sammy leans forward to talk to his brother, "Good Lord! This is the music these guys listen to?"

Coach Boots shrugs and shakes his head. The expletive's fly from Eazy-E's rap as he recounts the story of his gangster lifestyle. Sammy shakes his head and sighs, "Jesus, I'm getting old."

Chapter 38
The Road Less Traveled

Yankton, South Dakota, is a river city. It is located on the eastern bank of the Missouri River. It is a town of character. The original capitol of the Dakota Territory, there is history here, but the Old West stories are left for another day.

Located just below Gavins Point Dam and its reservoir, Lewis and Clark Lake, Yankton is just across the river from Nebraska. You head upstream from Yankton along the Missouri River, and you'll find the tree filled draws and breaks that were carved by the drainage over thousands of years. It's not as wild as it once was when the only inhabitants were the Yanktonai, or Sioux Indians, as they were later generically labeled. Yankton does not have the classic feel of a river city as a lot of the settlements lining the Missouri River do in North and South Dakota. Go farther north along the Missouri, and you will see the scenic bluffs looming over the cities. Even down stream there are towns and cities with more defined elevations and bluffs; most famously, Council Bluffs, Iowa. That's geology. The mouth of the James River empties into the Missouri in Yankton. This river, the "Jim River" as some call it, meanders the length of South Dakota and then some, all the way into North Dakota. The James River flows slowly and winds through some of the premier farm ground of the Dakotas. The history of time and water in the James River flood plain have flattened the surrounding area as well as deposited the fertile soils needed to produce the country's food supply.

What better place could the Reedville Cardinals Teener team be staying in their quest for a championship? There was none. This is where the base camp is established for the Reedville Teeners and their fans as they prepare their assault on the Town of Hutton in their pursuit for a state title.

The route chosen is a "short cut" as Coach Boots has deemed it. They get off the Interstate and begin heading cross-country on a series of paved county highways that slice through the fields of corn. The bus putters along the narrow, two-lane road leisurely making its way to

Yankton. It blocks an impatient driver, who honks alerting the bus to his presence. Chuck, seated in the back seat, shrugs at the honking car as he looked out the window of the rear emergency exit door. This prompts another prolonged hand on the horn from the car behind the bus. "Hey, everybody! Check this out!" Chuck hollers.

With the full attention of his teammates, Chuck drops the back of his shorts and presses his butt against the back window. Steady honks from the car behind the bus combine with howls of laughter from his teammates. "I hope they enjoy the view of a full moon!"

Chuck plays it up more than ever. He wiggles his butt some more in the window. The bus is jolted by a large pothole, sending everyone careening across seats. Chuck is propelled forward where he bounces off one seat back into the window. His butt slams into the glass sending a spider web crack radiating through the entire pane. Chuck finally falls forward onto the floor with his pants down. "H-h-h-h-holy shit!" Tony cries. "Y-y-y-you broke the window, Chuck!"

As everyone recovers from the pothole, they gather round to see the cracked window. Chuck recovers from the floor and fixes his britches. He looks at the broken window wide-eyed and laughs. "Oops," is his only comment.

The car behind the bus finally has room to pass and speeds by the side of the bus. The passenger and driver roll down their windows, stick out their arms, and extend their middle fingers as they pass.

At the front of the bus Coach Boots is hunched over the steering wheel, tired from the day's drive. The car passes honking and waving their middle fingers. Coach Boots waves at the car. "What the fuck is their problem?" he grumbles. "Not so friendly down here in our home country, eh Sammy?"

"Assholes, I guess," Sammy shakes his head droopy-eyed and sleepily. "We're foreigners in a hostile land."

"Ah, the memories," Coach Boots musters a smile as he catches his brother's eye in the mirror.

Chapter 39
Quarterfinals

Reedville, who is playing in the final game of the evening, has arrived a couple of hours in advance. There is a bit of nervousness, but mostly the six hour bus ride is the culprit for the lethargic warm-up the team experiences. The pregame ceremony commences, prompting the respective teams to assemble up and down the baselines and swear an oath of sportsmanship administered by an aging gentleman wearing his VFW jacket and hat. The Reedville Teeners sport their jerseys for the first time, adorned with black arm bands and patches with Coach Willis' initials on their uniforms. A few words are spoken in memory of the coach, a military veteran himself. The Star Spangled Banner is played over the loudspeakers, and the teams are ordered back to their dugouts as final field preparations are made by the grounds crew. The field is in pristine condition for the final game of the evening under the bright lights.

"Gather 'round!" Coach Boots calls the Reedville Teeners into the dugout as the team waits for the umpire to call, "Play Ball!"

The team presses around their coach. Coach Boots is stone-faced at first. "One more thing before we hit the field," he remarks as a smile slowly tugs at the corners of his mouth.

Coach Boots grabs the duffle bag next to him on the bench and pulls out a new batting helmet with a big bulls-eye hand painted on the top. Multiple arrows are painted on the helmet pointing to the bulls-eye. On the front painted in large, block letters is: "FIN".

"Fin, step up here," Coach Boots orders.

The team parts to make way for Fin to move up to Coach Boots' side.

"The old Coach had a pretty dry sense of humor. He had this helmet done up for Fin as a joke to break the tension for this first game. It was just a prop to make fun of poor Fin's bad luck and knack for getting beaned by more stray balls than anyone on a Teener team."

The smiles on the players faces turn into laughs. Coach Boots hands over the helmet to Fin. "If you don't mind Fin, I'd like you to wear it the first inning at least, to honor Coach."

Fin nods and accepts the helmet from Coach Boots. Donning the helmet, he is mobbed by his teammates as each player gets a slap on the bulls-eye atop the helmet. Jeers and cheers emanate from the dugout as the electricity of the game builds, and the umpires take their positions on the field. "All right, hands in!" Coach Boots yells out.

Coach Sammy's hand is first on his brother's, followed by the players hands piled on their coaches' hands. Coach Boots gives a nod, "On three, Cardinals! One, two, three!"

As Coach Boots calls out the number three, there is a roar from his team. "Cardinals!" echoes across the field.

The team bursts from the dugout to take the field amidst the cheers from the Reedville faithful. Under the lights the Reedville Teeners will play defense first to start their pursuit of a state championship.

* * * * *

Reedville is playing Parker in their opening round game. Parker is less than an hour away from Hutton, and the small town has rallied behind their Teener baseball team. The stands overflow, and the crowds spill down the sides of the field in standing room only positions along the foul lines.

Parker is just one of the numerous southeastern South Dakota farm towns that seem to blend together or are confused for one another. Parkston, Parker...what is the difference? The only discernible difference seems to be the mascot. Parker's mascot is the Pheasant; meanwhile, Parkston's is the Trojan.

The first two innings are all pitching and defense for Reedville behind Chuck. Three up, three down in succession with only one batter putting a ball in play, a foul out blooper to Tony at first base. The Parker pitcher matches Chuck's performance so far. With two out in the bottom of the second Dave comes to the plate. He digs into the batter's box, and the first pitch is delivered. Dave gets his money's worth on his swing. With a grunt he takes a mighty swat at the ball to no avail.

"Damn it!" Dave grumbles out loud to himself as he gathers himself from his whiff.

He chips away at the clay in the batter's box with his spike all the while shaking his head. He re-grips the bat and holds it with both hands high over his head as his eyes narrow, and he stares at the green lettering on the silver, metal bat: "Easton. Made in U.S.A."

He heaves a sigh and is ready to hit when a lone, female voice from the stands behind the plate whines, "Watch the ball all the way!"

"Time!" Dave calls out.

The umpire throws up his hands as the pitcher has just begun his wind up, but halts his throwing motion at the request for time. The catcher stands, and the umpire moves to sweep the dirt off the plate. Dave backs out of the batter's box and heaves a big sigh. He shakes his head, "What a brilliant idea! Watch the ball all the way!" Dave repeats the phrase mockingly.

Dave mumbles to himself some more and the opposing catcher gives him a wry smile as he meets Dave's eyes through his mask. "That your hitting coach up there in the stands?" Dave's opponent questions sarcastically as he squats into position behind the plate.

Dave stands, ready to hit staring at the pitcher. He answers his opposing catcher now squatting behind him, "Just one of my many adoring fans and critics."

The pitcher stares into the catcher, gets the sign, winds, and throws. Dave with his patented, power-swing uncoils and catches the pitch flush on the barrel of his bat. He drives it deep to straight away centerfield. As he moves out of the batter's box towards first base, he admires his work a little and shrugs before hustling around the bases. Dave rounds third base and is low-fived by Coach Boots from his third base coaching box. Boots yells to his catcher, "Thatta boy! Way to get us started! The slump is ova'!"

Dave crosses home plate and looks at the catcher and umpire standing behind the plate, assuring he touches home. Dave cocks his head and deadpans, "I guess I just need to watch the ball all the way."

The umpire and catcher both smile beneath their masks, and Dave's catching counterpart gives a congratulatory swat to Dave's behind as the big man heads to his dugout. His teammates have spilled out of their dugout, and Dave runs the gauntlet of congratulatory high fives and pats on the helmet. Sammy has moved from his first base coaching position and is the last to provide a double high five to Dave before returning to his coaching box.

The homerun is the opening of the floodgates for the Reedville offense, and the Cardinals chalk up eight more runs in the next three innings. In the bottom of the fourth, it is Tony at the plate. He takes a mighty hack at the Parker pitcher's offering and hits a dribbler down the third base line. It is a swinging bunt that the third baseman charges, bare-handing the ball, and flinging it, off-balanced, toward first base. Tony has hustled, but to no avail; the throw is offline and the first baseman is pulled from the base up the line toward home plate. He is able to tag Tony out, sweeping his glove across Tony's backside.

Dave is sitting next to Gary on the bench. They have leaned forward to observe the action on the field as Tony is tagged out. They relax and scoot back on their seats. Dave shakes his head, "He should've divven."

Gary looks at his friend, a puzzled expression contorting his face, "What?"

Dave edges forward on his seat on the bench. He is still replete with his catcher's gear, less his mask, as he waits in the dugout to go back on defense. He waves his arm toward fist base, "He should've divven. He probably would have gotten in under the tag."

Gary breathlessly laughs, "Divven? Let me guess...you're gonna be an English professor someday."

Dave laughs at his own ridiculously handicapped language. "What? Isn't 'divven' the past perfect participle tense...of 'dive'? It's somethin' like that, isn't it?"

Gary and Dave laugh out loud at their conversation. Tony returns to the dugout and stows his helmet. One by one each player on the team, starting with Gary, repeats the same phrase to Tony. Gary gives a nod to Tony, "Tony, you should have divven."

Fin is next, and he shakes his head, "I'm not an expert, but I would've divven."

Zach holds up his arms, one wrist still in a cast, mimicking a dive. "I woulda divven, but sometimes that could lead to injury."

Zach drops his good arm, just holding up his casted arm. He oversells a frown.

Chuck jumps in, "There's no doubt in my mind; I would have divven."

The laughter builds in the dugout. Turner is next, nodding his head. He simply states, "Divven."

Jesse shakes his head side to side, "You should've divven."

Lawrence clucks his tongue at Tony. "It was definitely a divven situation."

The bench is in riotous laughter at the ongoing joke. Tony looks around at the foolhardy laughers. He is clueless. He grabs a towel and wipes his sweaty face, "I-I-I-I know! I kn-kn-kn-know! I sh-sh-sh-should have d-d-d-d-divven!"

Everyone in the dugout roars with laughter garnering looks from Sammy at the first base coaching box, the first baseman in the field, as well as the pitcher on the mound.

"Wh-wh-wh-what the hell is so funny?" Tony yells, bewildered by the mayhem in the dugout.

Players are on their knees belly-laughing. They lie on the bench breathless with laughter.

Gary finally stands and clamps his hand down on Tony's shoulder. He points to Dave. "It's Dave. He's making up words to add to the dictionary. Today's word is 'divven'. Let me use it in a sentence for you: 'You should have divven into first base and avoided the tag."

Tony rolls his eyes and sits down on the bench, shaking his head still not understanding what is so funny.

Gary shrugs, "I guess you had to be there."

Tony still doesn't get it, "What?"

He looks at Gary who spins and moves back to his seat next to Dave. Everyone catches their breath and turns their attention back to the game.

The Reedville Teeners have returned to form. They have relaxed and score another six runs to put the ten-run-rule into affect as they breeze by Parker in the shortened five inning game fourteen to nothing.

The game ends, and the teams shake hands at home plate before returning to the dugout and sacking up the equipment. Coach Boots returns to the dugout after getting the instructions for the next game. He gathers the team around him in the dugout. "Good job tonight, boys. This is what we want. We want to be playing in the last game every night. Semi-finals tomorrow. Let's get out of here and get some rest."

The equipment is put away, goodnights are exchanged between parents and players, and the team is loaded on the bus. It is a raucous, victorious, ten-mile ride back to Yankton and the hotel for the evening. It is a quiet night in the hotel. The lessons learned from the region road trip are implemented without a warning.

The evening is over, but not for Gary. With a pocketful of change, he sets out for the payphone just outside of the hotel office. He deposits the coins and dials. The conversation is short and sweet, "Hi, Annie. We won. I wish you were here."

Annie's beaming smile almost comes through the phone, "That is awesome! I wish I was there too!"

Gary wraps up the conversation, "I got to go. I don't have much change. These stupid phones are expensive. See you later."

Annie whispers into the phone, "I know. Bye."

Chapter 40
Semifinals

The evening of Reedville's semifinal game finds the bleachers of the Hutton baseball field jam packed. The home town team, Hutton, plays the first game of the evening session and is victorious in beating the team from Underwood 12-9 in a hard fought battle. The home fans stay around to see who the local team is going face in the championship. It is standing-room-only in the stadium. The parking lot overflows, and cars line the streets in the residential areas as fans walk nearly a half mile from their vehicle to get to the ball park.

The semifinal matchup has its own back story. Reedville has an on-going rivalry with this night's opponent, Hot Springs. The Hot Springs Teeners had beaten or been beaten by Reedville in the last five consecutive years in the state tourney. The winner of the Reedville versus Hot Springs matchup is the odds-on favorite to be champion. The team that had the farthest distance to travel to the tournament, Hot Springs, has the preeminent baseball program west of the Missouri River in South Dakota for the last twenty years. With an energetic coach recently retired from Ellsworth Air Force Base at its helm, Hot Springs attracts the best players in the southwest corner of South Dakota. It is the matchup people want to see, northeast South Dakota versus southwest South Dakota.

All is calm and businesslike for the Reedville Teeners as the team finishes its warm up and settles into its dugout. It is Lawrence, the most unflappable player on the team, who is shaken as he looks across the field into the opposing team's dugout. Rudely pointing at the other dugout and stammering as he speaks, Lawrence, usually the calm, cool, and collected persona, is flustered. "D-D-D-Did you guys see this?" Lawrence stutters. "Holy Cow! They got a Black guy on their team. Check it out!"

It is Dave, just passing by Lawrence in the dugout, that stops and puts his arm around his teammate in an attempt to provide some calm. "That's ok," Dave comments reassuringly. "We got you, so let's call it a draw."

Dave lets go of Lawrence and moves through the dugout to find a seat on the bench. Lawrence is wound up. He grabs his jersey and tugs at his collar, "Guys," he shakes his head and whispers loudly in a very serious tone. "I'm not really Black! These chains," Lawrence pulls at the fake gold jewelry around his neck. "These chains aren't real gold! I'm not really a Black guy!"

Lawrence is worked up into a tizzy. Tony is annoyed by the outburst next to him and tries to defuse the situation. "Close enough," Tony comments. "Geez, Lawrence, relax."

Tony's sage words are not enough. Lawrence paces a bit staring into the far dugout. Shaking his head, he is incredulous. "I don't know how you can be so calm about this."

Lawrence takes a seat on the bench and rocks his body front to back, nervously looking across the field. It's Dave with a word painful to Lawrence's ears that brings the discussion to a halt. A nickname that Lawrence despises. "Let it go, Larry," Dave commands.

Lawrence begins to protest, "Hey..." He cuts himself off and smiles at Dave.

Dave returns the smile and a nod to the young hip-hopper, and the conversation about the opponent is finished just in time for the players to be called to the field for the oath of sportsmanship.

Returning to the dugout, Coach Boots signals his team to congregate around him in the dugout. He leans in to the huddle. "Gather 'round, everyone. Jus' like last night."

Coach Boots gives a nod to Sammy, "What's the word, Sammy?"

Sammy stoically replies, "Focus."

Coach Boots returns his attention to his team, "Focus. What's the other word, Sammy?" Bootsy again flips his gaze to his brother.

Sammy is quick to reply with his serious tone, "Concentrate."

Coach Boots nods as he looks at each player, "We can do this. Focus. Concentration. Seven innings of your undivided attention. That's all we are asking."

"All right," Coach Boots claps his hands. "Trent?" the coach nods affirmatively. "You ready to pitch?"

Trent puts his left hand on his right shoulder and rotates his arm, "Ready as I'll ever be."

Trent has confided in his coach that his arm is tired. His shoulder hurts, but he has tried to stay the course. Coach Boots points to Gary, "Gary, be ready. You'll be the first reliever, if necessary. Hands in everyone."

The coaches' hands are piled upon by their players. Coach Boots grits his teeth, "Let's go get 'em now! Cardinals on three! One, two, three!"

On the count of three the dugout rings with the cry of "Cardinals" as loud as anyone at the baseball stadium has ever heard the word screamed.

* * * * *

By the third inning it is all Hot Springs. Trent is struggling to throw strikes and finding little success with his aching arm. Reedville, at this point, is already down 8-2 with Chuck coming to the plate, leading off the bottom of the third inning. Chuck takes a mighty rip at the ball and grounds weakly to the third baseman, who promptly throws to first base getting a hustling Chuck out at first by a step. Chuck curls his path back to the dugout. "Damn it!" growls Chuck as he enters the dugout.

Slamming his batting gloves to the bench, he sits in disgust. Resting his head in his hands, he mumbles almost incoherently finishing with, "We're done."

Gary hears the words; they all hear the phrase vocalizing what everyone is thinking in the back of their minds. Gary is not going to accept it. "What did you say?" Gary asks through gritted teeth as he stands and approaches his teammate.

Gary towers over Chuck. Chuck is sitting on the bench, running his hands through his sweat-soaked hair, staring blankly at the dugout floor. Slowly Chuck turns his face toward Gary. He speaks with a pained whine, "I said, 'we're done.'"

Chuck, along with the rest of the dugout, flinches when Gary yells at the top of his lungs, "Get out of here!"

The blank look on Chuck's face is an honest expression of surprise and fear. He stares blankly at Gary. Gary extends his arm with his finger pointed at the boy, "You heard me. Get the hell out of this dugout before I throw you out. We don't need that attitude."

Chuck takes stock of his teammates. No one looks at him. Nobody comes to his defense, not even his best buddies, Turner and Jesse. He stands and slowly moves to the dugout steps and pauses. Gary raises his voice and growls, "Out!" Gary points and commands as if he were scolding a temperamental dog.

Chuck moves up the steps and out of the dugout, moving down the foul line away from home plate where he sulks, kicking at clumps of grass and watching the action on the field. Amidst the uproar of the dugout dispute, Lawrence has stepped up to the plate and run the count full. With three balls and two strikes, Lawrence lines a ringing single up the middle, just under the pitchers glove. Jesse follows Lawrence's single with a walk on four consecutive high and away pitches. The cheers from the dugout began to swell; the Reedville crowd is just itching to come to life with noise of support.

"Come on, Dave!" Coach Boots called out from his third base coaching box. "Ducks on the pond! Ducks on the pond!"

Coach Boots claps wildly as he shouts instructions to the base runners, listing the possible scenarios of a ball put in play. The catcher for Hot Springs has made a trip to the mound to calm down his pitcher, suddenly searching for the strike zone.

The Reedville dugout bounces with enthusiasm, seeking an elusive rally. Not lost on Chuck, the base runners draw him closer to the excitement exuding from the dugout. He moves adjacent to the dugout, leaning on the pole supporting the screen protecting the team. Chuck is clapping now, "Come on, Dave!" he shouts. "Come on, Dave!"

Gary glares at Chuck, but remains silent. Gary, along with the entire cadre in the dugout, is standing and leaning against the protective screen. The howls of contempt directed toward the Hot Springs pitcher and his ability to throw a strike rain down from the Reedville team. The pitcher smiles and gives a nod in the team's direction, sending the catcher back to his position behind the plate. Over the public address system, the announcement comes, "Now batting, the catcher, Dave Brown."

The crowd roars in anticipation for their power hitter. Dave digs in, and the pitcher, distracted by the base runners, continues to throw the ball high and outside, putting the count quickly at two balls and no strikes. Coach Boots calls into his hitter, "Pick out a good one. Put it in play."

The pitcher goes into his stretch, checks the runners, and delivers. It is the first strike in a while, and Dave is ready for it. The crowd is silenced momentarily by the ear-splitting clank of a ball off a metal bat's sweet spot. The quieted crowd gasps and explodes with a roaring cheer. The ball settles over the left field wall on a line drive path with fielders barely reacting to the shot off the "Big Stick" Easton bat. The dugout jumps, jostles, and the roughhousing celebration spills out onto the field to welcome home the three runs that cut the lead in half, making it suddenly a three run game. Chuck is the first player in line to welcome the players across home plate, having sprinted from his position at the far end of the bench, just outside of the dugout. "MVP! MVP!" Chuck chants loudly.

Chuck rejoins the dugout as the high-fives and celebrations wind down. Dave is back on the bench, reattaching his catcher's gear to his body. Shin guards on he leans back, grabs a towel, and wipes his sweat-streaked face. "Whew," he exhales. Throwing the towel aside, Dave elbows Gary, "Ya know what I shoulda done?"

Gary shakes his head and smiles, only imagining what Dave might say next. "What?"

"I should have divven into home when I crossed the plate," Dave remarks with an ultimate deadpan loud enough for everyone to hear.

A roar of howling laughter spills from the Reedville dugout, drawing curious looks from the crowd. Tony pops to right field for the second out, and Trent steps up to the plate, lining a shot at the shortstop, who stabs the ball, ending the inning. Trent flips the bat down and grabs at his right shoulder, rotating it for some relief to no avail. Coach Boots walks back to the dugout, having a conversation with Trent. The decision is made and Gary relieves Trent on the mound.

* * * * *

The next two innings put into the books by both teams were forgettable. Each team put up three runs making the score 11 to 8 in the bottom of the fifth. Lawrence is once again in the position of catalyst, leading off the inning. Gary attempts a pep talk as he puts his arm around the young hitter in the dugout before sending him out into the on-deck circle. He encourages his teammate, "Come on, Lawrence, show 'em how a Reedville Soul Brotha plays ball."

With a tap on the helmet and a shove out of the dugout propelling Lawrence to the plate, Gary is confident in the team's chances. On cue, Lawrence drives a solid single into right field, and the cheers from the dugout begin to rev up again. The momentum and cheers continue when Jesse follows with a solid single up the middle, putting runners on first and second with nobody out.

That was the end of the line for the Hot Springs pitcher. Relief is brought in to face Dave, but it is to little avail for the Hot Springs Teeners. Coach Boots is ready to take his coaching up a level from his third base coaching box. "Let's go, Dave," he emphasizes with a clap. "Level swing now. Line drive somewhere!"

It is advice heeded. Dave, taking a liking to the first pitch, gaps a line drive rope to left-centerfield. Lawrence scores easily, chains bobbing as he rounds third. Tucking his chains back in his shirt as he enters the dugout to high-fives, Lawrence beams. He is indeed the Reedville Soul Brotha.

Hot Springs changes pitchers again bringing in a different relief pitcher to try to quell the storm with score now 11 to 9, but runners are on second and third base, represented by Jesse and Dave. There is nobody out when Coach Boots calls time out as Turner digs into the batter's box. Coach and player meet halfway down the base line and have a chat. Hand covering his mouth to hide the conversation, Coach Boots advises his player, "Take a couple pitches up there. He's fresh in the game. I'm sure he's nervous with runners on base."

Turner nods, "Sure thing, Coach."

The advice is not really necessary; the first pitch sails inside and thuds off Turner's hip as he is unable to dodge out of the way. The bases are loaded for the other big man, Tony. Coach Boots claps and encourages, "Ok, Tone," Bootsy punctuates each word with a clap. "Drive the ball some place."

The crowd is beside itself with cheers. It is deafening behind the plate. The fresh pitcher works from the stretch position, checking the runners before delivering the pitch home. The first is a ball outside, then a ball skips in the dirt, and the Hot Springs catcher smothers the wild pitch preventing a run and holding the runners in their places. The count is two balls and no strikes, and the pressure mounts on the pitcher. With the bases loaded, there is no place to put the batter with a walk. Coach Boots points at his head as Tony looks down the third base line. "Be smart up there, Tony."

The pitcher sets and delivers. He grooves the pitch, trying to make sure of a strike. Tony is up to the task; he uncoils a mammoth swing on the straight fast ball down the middle. He drives the pitch over the center field wall in a monumental home run. The crowd goes bonkers as Reedville takes its first lead of the night 13 to 11.

In the dugout the Reedville Teeners are bouncing off the walls. The welcome-to-home-plate committee escorts Tony back to the bench. Adrenaline courses through everyone. Tony is pumped up. He paces like a caged lion up and down the dugout. He drinks a cup of water as he flexes. Zach is at his side wide-eyed as he checks out Tony's bicep. Fin is right in the mix. He pretends to have a camera and takes pictures as Tony models in body-builder poses.

"Grand Salami!" Fin yells. He gives Tony modeling direction, "Pout. Pout your lips. Flip your hair back."

Gary laughs along with his teammates as Tony poses. He shakes his head, "When did Teener baseball become Home Run Derby?"

Tony shrugs himself into another pose, "Wh-wh-wh-whadday mean? I b-b-b-been working out!"

Fin makes a fist and holds it near his crotch and moves it back and forth, simulating masturbation. "Yeah, Tone, we know your routine." Fin changes the motion to his other hand. "Look, Mom! I'm ambidextrous!"

Dave joins the fun. "Fin, I think you mean switch hitter."

Tony is mid-sip from his cup of water and does a spit-take as the revelry continues. The laughing and joking raucously escapes the dugout. The side is finally retired, and Gary returns to the mound with a smile, a lead, and a renewed determination.

* * * * *

For Gary the joy is short-lived as he struggles to throw strikes. Pitching with the lead hasn't changed his control issues. He labors on the mound, slowly contemplating each pitch. With one out and one on in the top of the sixth inning, Gary is muttering to himself as he stalks the pitching rubber. In the Reedville dugout, the comedy atmosphere fades as the attention turns to the defense and pitching. Coach Boots stands and casts his eyes toward his assistant coach. Sammy in turn casts his gaze on Fin and nods. "Fin, get some warm-up tosses in. We might need you," Coach Boots calls out over his shoulder while turning his attention back to the field.

Fin jumps from the dugout, and J.W. grabs a catcher's mitt. The pair moves down the foul line, and Fin warms up tossing the ball to J.W. The ball pops the catcher's mitt on each throw.

Coach Boots emerges from the dugout, calls timeout, and slowly ambles to the mound. The decision is never in question. Gary's eyes light up. He is relieved the coach is on his way out. Gary doesn't have it this evening, and he resigns himself to the fact that his pitching night is over.

Coach Boots finally reaches the mound meeting with Dave and Gary. It isn't much of a conversation. Coach Boots felt he might have more of an argument from the leader on the team, but the writing is on the wall. "How you feeling?" Coach Boots questions.

Gary is blunt. "Terrible. I can't throw a strike to save my life. I have no feel for the ball tonight."

Coach Boots heaves a sigh. "I got Fin ready. We'll pull Jesse, move you to left, and get Fin in here to close it out."

Gary gives a nod and hands the ball to his coach, "Sounds like a plan."

Coach Boots signals to Fin and summons Jesse from left field. Gary jogs off the mound toward left field. Jesse hustles in and high-fives Gary as they cross paths. Jesse continues to hustle off the field and high-fives Fin moving towards the mound. Jesse is met with a round of applause from the crowd and the dugout, and the showman in him makes him doff his cap.

Meanwhile on the pitcher's mound it is Coach Boots and his young pitcher along with the catcher discussing strategy. "You the man, Fin," Coach Boots begins. "Just like batting practice." Coach Boots waves a hand to the fielders. "The defense is right there behind you. Pitch to contact. Throw your usual strikes."

Oblivious to the pressure of the situation, it is a simple answer from Fin, "Sure thing, Coach."

Dave returns to his position at catcher, and Fin takes his warm up tosses. He finishes and the Hot Springs batter steps up to the plate to a hushed crowd. Before Fin gets into his stretch position, a cry comes from Gary in left field, "Ken-nee Ro-gers!" The phrase pierces the quiet air.

Laughter bursts from the Reedville dugout, and the players on the field, permeating the air. So much so, Fin has to laugh. His reflexive chortle causes his gum to fly from his mouth. He steps off the rubber and gathers himself. Fin moves over, picks up the dirty piece of gum, and starts to put it in his mouth. He thinks better of the maneuver as gasps from the crowd intermingle with cries of disdain from the dugout. Fin tosses the gum down and laughs at himself even more.

Attention is diverted back to Gary in left field, "Come on, Gambler!" Gary yells out from his distant position.

The giggles from the Reedville Teeners on the field and on the bench cannot be squelched. Gary's comment is quickly followed by Tony. "Come on, Kenny, make 'em fold 'em!"

Chatter from the infield and outfield rains down. Fin sets and fires. The Hot Springs batter lines to a diving Lawrence at second base, catching the ball on the fly. Lawrence gathers himself, stands and throws to first base, picking off the runner who has strayed too far. The side is retired on one pitch, and a roar goes up from the crowd while the Reedville players sprint from the field to the dugout, celebrating the third out on just a single pitch from Fin.

Reedville Teeners are back in the dugout with the side out. "Let's get some insurance runs!" Gary hollers.

Gary dons his helmet and batting gloves. High fives are still being exchanged, and the excitement is still high with victory so close. Out of the dugout pops Gary heading to the plate with a few practice swings as he watches the Hot Spring pitcher finish his warm up tosses. Gary leads off the inning with a double to the gap. Chuck follows with a single, and Gary scores. The early dugout feud is put to rest as Gary points to Chuck at first base, acknowledging the run batted in by his teammate. From his position on base, Chuck returns the point. Gary heads to the dugout. "That away, Chuck!" Gary pumps his fist. In the dugout Gary trades high-fives with everyone. He approaches Fin who is sitting on the bench with his jacket on trying to stay warm, "One more inning. Come on, Fin! We got an extra run for ya."

Fin is virtually oblivious to anything as he picks at his fingernails. "Uh, yeah," he looks up and sees Gary holding his hand up.

Fin slaps him five, "Three up, three down."

Reedville is retired, and Fin returns to the mound with a three run cushion up 14 to 11. It is the bottom of the seventh inning, the final inning for the semifinal game. Fin stands on the mound, smiling at the cheering crowd. Fin is as cool as a cucumber. He appears as if he is throwing batting practice as Coach Boots had advised. The first hitter of the inning digs into the batter's box. The initial pitch from Fin is a slow curveball on the outside corner. Coach Boots puts his hand on his heart, "Didn't I tell Fin to lay off the breaking balls?"

The second pitch is a fastball down the middle and the batter takes it for a called strike. Fin winds and fires again working quickly. He lays a slow breaking pitch on the outside corner.

In the dugout Coach Boots winces as he watches the slow pitch lined down toward right field as the hitter waits back nicely and tags it with an inside out swing. Coach Boots and the rest of the team on the bench twist trying to use body English as the ball zips toward Tony. He leaps and catches it. "Hey!" Coach Booths jumps to his feet. "Tony, way to sky!"

Tony throws the ball around the horn, starting with Trent at shortstop. Trent tosses to Lawrence at second base, and finally from Lawrence to Aric at third base. Aric returns the throw to Tony who is approaching the mound. Tony gloves the ball as he moves next to Fin. He hands the ball to a smiling Fin. "Nice grab," Fin says. "I swear, we probably could have gotten two sheets of paper under your feet."

Fin holds his thumb and forefinger together with no separation. "You were up high, Big Man."

Tony shakes his head as he turns to move back to his position at first base. "Just keep throwing strikes, Kenny Rogers."

Fin laughs and drops the ball from his glove. He scrambles after the ball rolling off the slope of the pitcher's mound. Fin gathers the ball and looks around sheepishly. He returns to the pitching rubber and gets the sign from Dave behind the plate. The hitter is fooled badly on two consecutive breaking balls in the dirt and is quickly down no balls and two strikes. The third pitch is a high fastball, and the batter pops it straight up over home plate. Dave flips his mask away, puts his back to the infield, and makes the catch. The crowd cheers wildly, sensing the end is near. Dave fires the ball to Tony, throwing the ball around the horn to celebrate the out.

Coach Boots calls time and moves to the mound where he meets Fin and Dave. The crowd has calmed a bit, but cheers of "Let's-Go-Reedville" echo through the bleachers. "You okay, Fin?" Coach Boots asks.

Fin shrugs, surprised at the question, "Sure."

"Just enjoy the moment. Listen to the crowd cheer." Coach Boots counsels as his eyes scan the crowd.

Fin searches the crowd. "It is kinda awesome." Fin tosses the ball back and forth into his glove.

A big grin forms on Coach Boots' face and is reflected by both Dave and Fin. He gives Fin a pat on the butt. "One more thing; lay off the breaking balls a little. You're going to give me a heart attack the way you lob that spinner up there."

Fin and Dave chuckle, and Coach Boots jogs back to the dugout. Dave gives Fin a pat on the butt with his glove. "Hey now, this is their leadoff guy, so bring your good stuff."

Fin nods. The batter is announced, "Now batting for Hot Springs, the center fielder, Lyle Snell."

Dave returns to his position behind the plate and gives the signal for a fastball. The hitter swings and drives a sinking liner to left field. Gary sprints in and picks the ball off his shoe top on a dead run. The game is over. He keeps his momentum and runs all the way to the mound to congratulate Fin. Gary delivers a congratulatory slap on the back. "I knew we could count on somebody with a nickname of 'The Gambler'."

Gary gives Fin a high five and hands him the ball. "Keep the ball as a souvenir."

The teams meet at home plate and exchange handshakes before returning to their respective dugouts. Hot Springs is devastated in contrast to the opposite dugout, the Reedville Teeners are flying high.

They listen to the final instructions for the night provided by Coach Boots. "Great game tonight! Great game! The best comeback under pressure I have ever seen!"

Coach Boots smiles a big toothy grin; in an instant the joyous expression disappears, replaced by the serious expression of a funeral preacher. "But, we're not done. Get some rest tonight when we get back to the hotel. Get to bed. No horsing around."

The players nod in agreement. Coach Boots continues. "Tomorrow night we are up against the home team, Hutton. The crowd will definitely be in their favor."

Coach Boots' smile broadens. "All right, get your hands in. Cardinals on three. One, two, three!"

The entire team has their hands in and bellows, "Cardinals!" The echo booms across the empty stadium.

The team sacks the equipment and heads to the bus as their home town fans and parents provide congratulations and send them on their way to the hotel.

Chapter 41
Downtime

The morning of championship game day finds the Reedville Teeners hanging by the pool of the Yankton Cedar Breaks Motor Lodge. The accommodations are nice. The hotel pool area has a hot tub and shuffleboard court where friendly competition between players gets a little heated with excessive trash talking. Tony enjoys the hot tub while he keeps an eye on the shuffleboard game, waiting for his turn. "Hey everybody! Check it out! It's like a dream come true!" Tony cries out, starved for attention.

Tony sits in the hot tub with his trunks expanded to the hilt by the bubbles. He points proudly to his full trunks with both hands out of the water. His smile is wiped from his face in a flash when he spies Fin, wearing a Speedo, staring down at him. "Nice," Fin nods.

Tony's face is twisted in an expression of disgust and fascination. "Holy crap, Fin! That is a large bulge ya got there in your trunks."

Fin perks up, "Thanks for noticing!"

He reaches into his tight Speedo. Tony's eyes widen, and he ducks away shielding his eyes. "What are you doing? I don't wanna see that!" Tony cries turning his head away.

Fin removes a baseball from his swimsuit. "What's your problem? It's just a baseball." Fin flips the ball up in the air and catches it with his right hand. He grips the seams in various positions. "I'm working on the grip of my new pitch, a knuckle curve. I'm keeping a baseball with me at all times, so I can get the feel."

Several players grab Fin and haul him toward the pool. "What are you doing?" Fin cries shrilly as he struggles to free himself. "I can't swim! No!"

The ball falls from Fin's hand. He is in full panic mode. Aric wrestles Fin's kicking leg. "Fin, nobody in America wears a Speedo. You gotta be dunked. Take that shit back to Europe."

"No! I can't swim!" Fin continues his wailing.

"On three," Aric commands. "One," the gang of players swings Fin in rhythm. "Two. Three!"

Fin flies into the pool screaming. "Help! Help me!" he cries.

Fin splashes and flails, "Help!"

The players laugh and point at the hapless Fin.

"Please help!" Fin pleads from the pool.

Dave stares down at the blonde boy. "Fin, the water's like four feet deep. Stand up!"

The screams and the splashing cease. Fin stands up in the shallow water. "Oh. Never mind."

Chapter 42
The Pep Talk

Dusk falls, and the Reedville Teeners make the bus ride from Yankton to Hutton. They arrive on the field and follow the routine of the previous two days. The team plays catch to warm up. It is a quiet session as the lines of players toss the balls back and forth with little conversation. The third and fourth place game is taking place before the championship game, and, once the players are warm, they take time to watch Hot Springs and New Town compete. The third place game ends with a Hot Springs victory, and the field is made ready for the final game. Players continue their warm up with a few sprints in the outfield and a little more catch.

The crowd packs into the bleachers. The hometown Hutton Teeners have the full support of the community, outdoing the Reedville faithful, but not by much. The players are introduced one by one, and they stand on the baselines where they take the sportsmanship oath and sing along to the national anthem.

The umpires send the teams back to their respective dugouts as the grounds crew makes the final preparations to the field. Coach Boots has gathered the team in the dugout for his final pep talk. Before he can say anything, he is interrupted by a voice from outside the dugout. It is the Hutton Teeners' Coach, Alex Chambers. "Good luck tonight, fellas." Alex states with all the sincerity of a snake oil salesman. "You too, BJ. How's it going my Home Boy?" Alex gives a nod to Coach Boots, "It's been long time, Booth."

Alex Chambers is all grown up now, if you could call it that. The boy that tortured an overweight BJ as a child never really matured. To make matters worse, Alex never physically grew much. His short stature gives him a chip on his shoulder that Napoleon would envy.

Coach Boots looks up at the opposing coach. The flood of memories comes washing over him. All the bullying, all the torture Alex put him through takes Boots back to his childhood. "Yeah. It has, Alex," Coach Boots mumbles.

It's Tony that elbows Dave and whispers, "D-D-D-Did he just call him BJ?"

Coach Boots turns his head ever so slightly, having overheard Tony's whispering. "Yes, Tony. This is where I grew up. My name is Bobby Jim. Everyone called me BJ for short."

Tony shrugs and makes a face, "Huh. I n-n-n-never knew that. K-K-K-Kinda explains things."

Tony opens his mouth, makes a fist, and moves it back and forth near his mouth. Coach Boots, his back to Tony, cannot see what's going on. The dugout ripples with snickers and giggles. The Hutton coach smiles, observing Tony's simulation.

"I know what you're doing, Tony. So, just knock it off."

Tony stops immediately trying to understand how Coach Boots knew. His arms are pinned at his sides, and he puts on a face of innocence. Before anything else can come of it, the Hutton coach leans over the dugout rail, raising his hand; he wags an admonishing finger at the team. "I'll tell you one thing; when we get you down tonight, there will be no big comeback like you had against Hot Springs."

The Reedville players stare at the Hutton Coach in disbelief as he waves a finger back and forth pointing at the group and smiling menacingly. The threatening presence of the coach falls harmlessly away as he wishes the best to the team with a sing-songy, "Ok, good luck."

Coach Boots is stunned to silence by the disruption from his opposing coach. He finally manages to grunt, "Uhhh, yeah."

The Hutton coach turns and jogs back across the field, headed toward his own dugout. Coach Boots stares at the small man running away, "Yeah, jog away, ya jackass."

The team sits in silence at the bizarre event that had unfolded so quickly in front of their eyes. Coach Boots turns and faces his team. The puzzled looks on his players' faces say it all. He points a thumb over his shoulder at the opposing team's dugout. A wry smile paints Bootsy's face, "Well, thank you, gracious host team."

Sammy chimes in, "They ain't no fucking Martha Stewart."

The comment brings out a bit of nervous laughter from the team, but it's Chuck's outburst that gets everyone's attention. He stands and with the energy of a coiled spring, he explodes, "Let's kick their asses!"

The shout quells the din from the crowd momentarily; every head in the packed bleachers glances toward the Reedville dugout before conversations return and the buzz of a thousand voices recommences.

Coach Boots can't help but giggle. He holds up a hand in Chuck's direction and puts on his best serious face. "Chill out a moment, Chuck."

Chuck is still standing in the dugout poised to fight. He nods and backs to his seat on the bench and flops down. He frowns in a reconciliatory expression, "Sorry."

Coach Boots makes the most of a dramatic pause. He sweeps his eyes over the players before him. He catches Sammy's eye and receives a nod from his brother. He clears his throat, "I want you to know that I'm very proud of you all, and I am very proud to be here with you."

Coach Boots reaches to the back pocket of his uniform and pulls some folded papers out and holds them above his head. He straightens the battered papers, the edges slightly frayed. The creases refuse to yield as the Coach struggles to unfold the papers.

"Anybody know what this is?" Coach Boots poses the question. "Anyone?"

Silence stills the dugout. Coach Boots hands the stack of papers to Dave. "This is a very treasured item to me. This is my copy of the minor league contract I signed. Go ahead, pass it around. Take a look at it."

Dave flips a couple pages and hands it off. Coach Boots continues, "Those papers with the Iowa River Dogs represent a dream come true." Coach Boots waves a hand, indicating to keep the papers moving. He smiles, "Funny thing is, sometimes a person has more than one dream. I struggled being away from you guys and this team. Of course," Coach Boots holds up the cast on his left hand, "when you break your wrist, and you start your career hitting two for twenty, maybe you're not quite cut out for pro ball."

The papers circulate through the team. "I learned a lot in just fifteen days as a person paid to play baseball. I would do it all again the same. But, I found out this is what I want to do. I want to be a coach like Coach Willis."

The players in the dugout are frozen. Mesmerized by Coach Boots, they are riveted to his speech, hanging on every word. "See, guys, the truth is I was kind of overweight as a kid. I wasn't a very good Little Leaguer...right here...in the town of Hutton. Like I said, I was a chubby kid."

Coach Boots looks in the direction of Tony and Dave. Tony can't resist, "Why you lookin' at us?" Tony turns to Dave, "He's looking at us, isn't he?"

Dave nods, and a few giggles scatter through the team, drawing smiles from Coach Boots and Sammy. "You see," Coach Boots continues pointing to the opposing dugout, "that head coach for Hutton over there; we were on the same Little League team. He used to beat me up. He said I was hurting the team. He tried to bully me into quitting baseball." The words cause Coach Boots to choke up a bit. He clears his throat and takes a deep breath. He doesn't make eye contact with the team; he stares at the back wall of the dugout, a far away look in his eyes. "My Little League coaches didn't do anything to help me. I could have easily quit. But I love baseball, everything about it."

Coach Boots pauses and nods his head slightly as he takes in the faces of the players staring back at him. "You guys could've quit. When we had a few injuries." Everyone glances at Zach a moment, and Coach Boots continues. "When we stunk at the conference tourney. When you had the motel trouble at regions. We all had plenty of excuses to quit"

There is a bit of shuffling caused by discomfort of the memory of the police showing up at the hotel at the regional tourney. Coach Boots shakes his head, "You had all the reason in the world to quit when Coach Willis passed away. Hell, when I heard the news in Iowa, I felt like quitting baseball."

Coach Boots points a finger at the team and sweeps it back and forth, "But we didn't quit!" His voice rises, fiery now. "You go out there tonight and give it all you got, and win or lose, you can be proud of what you've done!" Coach Boots is nearly shouting, "I am proud of you all, win or lose!" Coach Boots winds down a bit with a deep breath, "That's all I ask of you tonight. Just give it all you got."

It is deathly quiet for a moment as the words sink in. Coach Boots puts out a hand in the direction of Chuck, raising his eyebrows, "Chuck?"

Chuck leaps from his position on the bench and waves a towel as he shrieks, "Let's kick their asses!"

"Get your hands in here," commands Coach Boots. "Cardinals on three. One, two, three."

With hands piled high, squeezing everyone together in the dugout, the howl of "Cardinals!" reverberates through the dugout spilling out onto the field and once again causing the crowd to pause to see what the commotion is all about.

"Line up!" Tony cries as the team un-piles from their cheer. "Line up and get your eye-cock! It's the ceremonial application of the eye-cock!"

What has become a lucky ritual for the team, and likely the final time for many of the players, everyone lines up like a church communion with Tony managing the role of priest. First in line is Gary. Tony holds the applicator in folded hands and bows slightly. He grabs the tube of eye black like a pencil and draws a line under each of Gary's eyes while reciting the oath, "May the eye-cock go with you..."

Gary nods and takes the eye-black applicator and lines each of Tony's cheeks, returning the oath, "...and with you."

With a slight bow Gary hands the eye-black back to Tony who proceeds to draw the black greasy lines on each player's cheek. Gary approaches Coach Boots. "You in, Coach?"

Coach Boot shrugs, mystified by the line of players. "What the hell are you guys doing? And what the hell is eye-cock?"

Gary chuckles, "It's just eye-black. You know how Tony is. God only knows what's going on in that kid's head. Are you in or what?"

Coach Boots smiles, "Let's do it! Sammy, get over here! We got to get our eye-cock on!"

Coach Boots and Sammy wait at the back of the line and receive their marks of eye-black on each cheek. High fives are provided to the coaches by their players.

Chapter 43
Championship

Fin's hot hand got him the starting pitcher designation for the game. His effectiveness the evening prior and his limited pitch count prompted Coach Boots to give the nod to the "Blonde Bomber" as he was quickly becoming known to his teammates and the crowd. His white hair and dominance nearly supplanted the moniker of "Kenny Rogers" he had been earlier designated.

The home team of Hutton is meeting all the hype. The Sioux Falls local television station covers the team and its home town hosting duties. So far, Hutton is up to the task on the night. Hutton claims the early victory. They win the coin toss and are designated the home team. They are in the field first and get the last at bat. It is fitting for the magical season they are having. The Hutton Teeners, the Bulldogs, had been a force in the regular season, compiling a record of 32 wins and five losses. All the losses had been to the Sioux Falls Teener teams, a much higher level of competition than the Class B Teener level.

Play begins, Reedville and Hutton both go down in order in the first inning. The offenses are slow starting, especially Reedville. Coach Boots is second guessing his designation of Fin as the starting pitcher in the bottom of the second inning. Fin makes good pitches, but Hutton hitters make even better swings in stringing together four straight hits, plating two runs. Fin retires the side, but Coach Boots pulls Gary discreetly aside in the dugout and tells him to be ready in relief. Trent, the ace of the staff in the regular season, has resigned his pitching duties for the year. His shoulder aches and he is unavailable to pitch.

The top of the third inning leaves Reedville's bats still quiet. Hutton continues to bunch hits together and two more runs are scored. After three full innings, it is a 4-0 lead for the home town Hutton Bulldogs, and the screams and cheers of the Hutton faithful match the anticipation of a long-awaited championship. It is still early, but the Hutton left-handed pitcher, Franky Chase, is dominating. They call him "The Hammer," but he is more like a different tool, a scythe. He mows down all Reedville hitters with superior fastballs, pinpoint control, and a devastating curveball. The left-hander gives up only two hits in the first four innings. In the bottom of the fourth inning it is the end of the line for Fin's pitching day. A two run blast, a home run drives Fin from the mound, prompting Gary in relief. The Hutton coach goes wild from his third base coaching position, inciting the crowd with leaps, hollers, and gyrations as the Hutton fans go crazy.

Gary shuts the door on Hutton for the rest of the inning, and the top of the fifth shows the scoreboard tally Hutton 6, Reedville 0.

Coach Boots gathers his team in the dugout before taking his position in the third base coaching box. "Ok, guys," the coach paces in front of his team. "It's the top of the fifth inning. We got this at bat and two more. We're runnin' out of innings."

He talks quickly and firmly as his pacing continues. "Chuck, you're pitching the rest of the way. You got to shut 'em down buddy."

Chuck stands at attention and salutes. "You got it coach," he says resolutely.

Coach Boots turns to Sammy, "Who we got up?"

Sammy stands, "We got Gary up, Chuck on deck, and Tony in the hole."

"Let's get some runs!" Coach Boots commands with authority as he pumps his fist, turns, and leaps up the dugout steps, breaking into a run toward his position in the third base coaching box.

"You heard him!" Sammy repeats. "Get some runs!"

* * * * *

Gary digs in at the plate. His confidence is high after having seen the lefty's best stuff earlier. He figures the guy has to be getting tired by now, and he is right. The Hutton lefty rocks and fires; he flinches as the ball leaves the bat faster than the pitch is delivered. The ball hops to the fence in the left-centerfield gap, and Gary digs for extra bases. He slides into third base just ahead of the throw. Coach Boots picks himself up from the ground after trying to make sure Gary receives the signal to get down by prostrating himself on the ground. The Coach brushes the soil from his uniform in tandem with Gary as he approaches the base containing his player. The Reedville crowd finally has something to cheer about and goes crazy over the leadoff triple by Gary.

Coach Boots moves to Gary's side, "You didn't see my trying to hold you at second base?"

Coach Boots is aggravated by Gary not following his coaching, but he composes himself. Gary holds up his hands, "The play was in front of me. It was a triple all the way."

Coach Boots shakes his head and pats Gary on the rear, "Good job!" He gives Gary a nod as he backs into his coaching box and offers more coaching. "Watch the passed ball! We need your run to break the ice!"

Coach Boots words are from his lips to God's ears. Chuck is barely dug into the batter's box, and the big lefty, working from the stretch position, a rare occasion this evening, coils and uncorks a pitch right at Chuck's feet. Chuck skips rope over the ball and backs away as the wild pitch caroms by the catcher going to the backstop. Gary breaks to the plate instantly and scores the first run of the game for Reedville without a throw. High fiving Chuck on the way to the dugout, even over the roaring Reedville faithful, Gary can hear his coach yelling, "Good job, G Mann!"

The run-scoring wild pitch brings the Hutton coach out of his dugout for a visit to his starting pitcher. Coach Alex Chambers walks slowly to the mound arriving well after the Hutton catcher has made it to the pitching rubber. The conversation lasts all of 15 seconds. "You all right?" Coach Chambers asks his pitcher.

Franky is expressionless. "Yup," he responds.

"All right then," Coach Chambers swats his pitcher on the butt and walks off the mound as deliberately as he arrived, measured steps, eyes focused on the ground in front of him. His mind never even considered that his big horse of a pitcher wouldn't finish the game as the winning pitcher. This was just a visit for Franky to catch his breath. The Reedville crowd has started to believe. They chant in unison, "Reed-ville! Reed-ville!" steadily now.

With the catcher back in place behind the plate, Chuck digs in and laces the next pitch to the gap for a double. Coach Boots yells from his coaching box, "That-a-way, Chuckie! On the base! On the base." He holds up two arms high, giving the sign to Chuck to stay on second.

The Reedville fans are on their feet stomping and cheering. Nobody out and a man on second, this is the rally they were waiting for. Tony comes to the plate and grounds a ball up the middle where the second baseman makes an outstanding fielding play to throw out Tony at first. With average speed Tony would have been safe, but the big man, even with his hustle, is out. The ground out pushes Chuck to third base with one out in the inning. Coach Boots acknowledges Tony's effort. "It's ok, Tone! Good hustle!"

Coach Boots is excited now. The momentum seems to shift with the one run the Cardinals have plated, "Come on, Law-Dog," Coach Boots calls out through cupped hands for a megaphone effect.

Lawrence steps to the plate with confidence. He works the count to two balls and one strike, getting in a hitter's count. Franky Chase has worked himself into a lather at this point. He is sweating this inning out metaphorically and literally, but he rises to the occasion and delivers a pitch that Lawrence pops to the second baseman for the second out. The cheers swing immediately from Reedville fans back to the home town Hutton crowd.

Dave stands in the on-deck circle where he unsnaps the final straps of his shin-guards and moves to the batter's box to cheers and jeers from fans of both teams. Coach Boots claps and points to Chuck at third base. "C'mon, now! C'mon, Dave! We need this run at third base!"

Dave settles into the box and takes a fastball strike from the lefty. Once again, a divided crowd both celebrates and scoffs at the call. Dave steps out, takes a deep breath, and adjusts his batting gloves. In the dugout Gary observes out loud while sipping his cup of water, "He's going to take him deep."

Next to Gary, Zach sits keeping the scorebook. He concurs with Gary's premonition, "I wouldn't doubt it."

They are wrong. It's something more devastating than a home run. Dave steps back in the box, and the pitcher wastes no time getting set and delivering. The fastball from the big lefty doesn't tail like he wants. The ball zips with velocity straight across the heart of the plate, and Dave is ready with his power swing. The ball is lined straight back on the same plane as it left the pitcher's hand. The ball catches the pitcher flush on the kneecap as he follows through in a vulnerable off balance position about fifty-five feet from home plate. Franky Chase, star left-handed pitcher collapses in a heap, the ball ricocheting away and dribbling toward the Hutton dugout. Chuck scores and Dave legs out a hit. Before the Reedville faithful and players can muster a cheer, the sickening sound of the ball off the knee squelches any exhilaration. All attention is focused on the health of the Hutton pitcher, writhing in pain at the bottom of the mound. The Hutton coach springs from his dugout to aid his pitcher. A smattering of applause begins as Franky Chase is up trying to walk off the blow to his knee, but his pronounced limp speaks volumes.

With umpires and coaches watching, Franky climbs back on the mound to make a few tosses to his catcher and evaluate whether he can continue. Three warm-up pitches later and a dozen deep knee bends, the big lefty declares he is ok to go. He waves coaches back to the dugout and umpires back to their positions. Fin is at the plate ready to hit with Dave on first base, two out, and Reedville down four runs. Coach Boots hollers from his position, stopping the action before it even starts, "Time out!"

Coach Boots beckons Fin down the third base line. They meet halfway and Coach Boots advises, "Make him throw you a strike."

"Will do," Fin replies stepping, back to the plate as he takes two momentous practice swings.

The practice swings are for show. Fin doesn't take the bat off his shoulder and watches four straight pitches out of the strike zone, earning a base on balls.

The crowd revs up again, half cheering and half howling foul regarding the umpire's calls. It is Turner to the plate with the same advice from Coach Boots, and with an identical result. The back-to-back walks load the bases for light-hitting Jesse.

It is bedlam in the crowd. The Hutton coach starts up the dugout steps and puts a foot out of the dugout. Franky Chase waves his glove at his coach and shakes his head from side to side, and the coach backs down into the dugout. Coach Alex Chambers paces as he watches his ace out on the mound and can feel the tide turning.

Jesse steps to the batter's box and looks down the third base line to his Coach. "Make him throw you a strike!" Coach Boots hollers.

Jesse nods and steps in the box. The clank of the metal bat on the ball silences the crowd. The entire stadium had expected Jesse to follow his previous batters in taking a couple pitches, making the pitcher work to throw a strike. It had never occurred to Jesse to not swing at a strike. He got a ball in the middle of the plate, and he turned on it, lashing the pitch down the third base line. It is a bases clearing double that Coach Boots jumps back from as it sizzles eye-high down the line in front of him. He waves all the runners in to score and signals Jesse to hold on second base. Coach Boots quickly follows his stop sign to Jesse with a shrug of the shoulder as he calls across the field, "Way to make him throw you a strike!"

The last Reedville runner hasn't even touched home plate, and the Hutton coach is out of the dugout on his way to the mound. A day late and a dollar short, Alex Chambers holds his head down; he slowly walks to the mound, stunned at the deafening cheers of the Reedville crowd and devastating turn of events. Coach Chambers calls in his left fielder to pitch and signals to the dugout for a replacement left fielder. Coach

Chambers takes the ball from his ace-lefty's hand and places it in the reliever's, while putting his hand on the shoulder of his wounded pitcher. They walk off the mound together. Heads hanging low, Franky limping profusely, the pair moves to the dugout with a stirring round of applause behind their departure.

The new Hutton pitcher completes his allotted warm-up pitches, and Trent steps to the plate. On one pitch, Trent grounds to the shortstop who throws to first for the third out of the inning, and the side is retired in the bottom of the fifth. The inning is over, but the momentum has decidedly swung to Reedville, down only one run now: Hutton 6 and Reedville 5.

* * * * *

The spring in the step of the Reedville Teeners gives them the appearance of a different team. Chuck takes to the mound as a man possessed. Rocking and firing as quickly as Dave can return the ball from his catcher's position, Chuck strikes out the side in the bottom of the inning. The Hutton lineup sees only twelve pitches, nine of them strikes, and the side is out. Chuck leisurely strolls from the mound as he enjoys dropping a curveball into the dirt for the final strike and strikeout of the inning. Dave blocks the ball in the dirt and tosses the ball to Tony at first to confirm the out. Reedville Teeners hustle all around Chuck back to the dugout as he takes his time, enjoying himself all the way back to the bench.

* * * * *

Before Coach Boots heads to his third base coaching position, he gathers his players in the dugout. "We got the top of our line up again. Let's put this game away right now. Let's get some runs!"

Sammy is caught up in the excitement, "They ain't the same team without their good pitcher! Let's step on their throats and piss all over their hometown celebration!"

"Hear, hear!" Chuck echoes.

"Hands in here," Coach Boots orders. "Cardinals on three. One, two, three!"

With all hands in, the cheer explodes out of the dugout, blasting louder than the cheering crowd.

Coach Boots and Sammy pop out of the dugout and sprint to their respective coaching positions. Gary leads off the inning against the inferior pitcher that replaced the lefty. He singles, bringing Chuck to the plate. Chuck works the count to three balls and one strike. The hitter's count affords him to be selective, and he singles, driving Gary to third base. With nobody out, Tony steps to the plate. He takes a ball, high, and Chuck steals second base. Runners now at second and third, the Hutton coach moves from the dugout. He signals to the shortstop, and Hutton makes a pitching change, swapping the pitcher and the shortstop. After the pitcher's warm up tosses, Tony steps back to the plate with a one ball no strike count. The first pitch is stroked for a single by Tony plating both Gary and Chuck. The two runs give Reedville the lead for the first time in the game, Reedville 7 and Hutton 6 as the Reedville faithful go wild.

Lawrence follows Tony with a walk, putting runners on first and second with nobody out and drawing Dave to the plate. From the dugout Chuck begins shouting, "M-V-P! M-V-P! Come on, everyone!"

The dugout joins in the chant much to the chagrin of Dave. He steps out of the batter's box unable to hide his smile. He takes a couple of practice swings and steps back up to the plate. Coach Boots shouts instructions to the base runners, "Watch the line drive! Don't get doubled off!"

Dave focuses on the pitcher now. He is oblivious to any noise in the outside world except for his own breathing. The pitcher delivers, and Dave is out front on his swing. He hits a long foul ball down the left field line. Very deep and very foul, the crowd collectively draws its breath momentarily, imagining a home run. It is just a long strike, and Dave is in a hole, no balls and two strikes. Coach Boots provides the coaching, "Straighten it out, Big Man!" He punctuates the "Big Man" with two big claps.

The pitcher gets another ball from the umpire and strolls around the mound wiping his brow with his short sleeve shirt, finally climbing back on top of the hill and stepping on the rubber. Dave takes a deep breath and readies for the next pitch as the pitcher checks the runners at first and second base. It's a fastball, but this pitcher is no match for the Reedville hitters. Dave is ready and unleashes a mighty blast that is a "no doubter." The left fielder doesn't move but watches the ball sail over the fence. The Reedville dugout is on its feet at contact; they hold their breath an instant before a collective cheer goes up realizing it is a home run. Dave rounds the base without a hint of a smile. It's all business for him. Dave greets his RBI base runners he has driven in with high fives at the plate. Back to the dugout Dave trots; it is the silent treatment for Dave as he looks for someone to high five, but no one offers a hand. The dugout pretends nothing has happened for a good fifteen seconds before exploding in cheers and piling on Dave as he sits on the dugout bench reattaching his shin-guards.

Reedville tacks on two more runs before they are finally retired in the top of the sixth inning where the scoreboard indicates Reedville 12 and Hutton 6.

* * * * *

Chuck is back on the mound for the bottom of the sixth inning. Every pitch is cheered as Chuck works quickly, winding and firing strike after overpowering strike at the Hutton batters. The first hitter of the inning is jammed and grounds weakly off the handle of the bat to Tony at first base. Tony fields the ball and steps on the base for the first out. The second Hutton batter works the count full off Chuck before looping a pop out off the handle to Trent at shortstop. The third hitter of the inning is overmatched, and three fastballs are powered by his bat for an inning ending strikeout. The Reedville fans in the crowd get to their feet. Chuck walks off the mound, raises his arms, and motions for more noise as he moves toward the dugout.

* * * * *

The Hutton Teeners are still searching for a pitcher. Nothing has gone in their favor since losing their star pitcher. They change pitchers again to no avail. Reedville scratches together two more runs and when the final out of the top of the seventh inning is recorded, the scoreboard shows the Reedville Cardinals with a comfortable eight run lead, Reedville 14 and Hutton 6.

* * * * *

Chuck takes the mound for the bottom of the final inning, and he picks up right where he left off. He drops down to a sidearm fastball, and the Hutton batter swings and misses, striking out. Chuck goes back to the well one too many times. Dropping down sidearm again on the next batter, he sticks the pitch right in the hitter's ribs. The crowd provides a collective gasp at the dull thud of the batter hit-by-pitch. The hitter shrugs off the pain and walks, slightly bent to the side of the battered ribcage, but he finds himself on first base. The Hutton crowd can feel the inkling of a rally and picks up its cheering. The roller coaster ride of emotion for Hutton continues. The next batter swings and misses at a ball in the dirt for a third strike, but the wild pitch scoots by Dave to the backstop and the suddenly sour strikeout turns into runners at first and second with one out. Hutton fans ride the exciting crest of thoughts of a comeback.

Coach Boots calls timeout. He heads to the mound and meets with Chuck and Dave. The conversation is short and one-sided. "Relax, gentlemen. Focus on the hitter. That's it. Let's wrap this baby up."

Coach Boots swats his pitcher on the behind and jogs back to the dugout, leaving Dave and Chuck at the mound. "Fastballs?" Dave queries his pitcher.

"Yeah, let's stick with all fastballs," Chuck agrees as Dave turns and steps away. "Hey," Chuck calls his catcher back. "Just go through the signs. I'll shake you off on everything, but it'll still be all fastballs."

Dave nods and jogs back to his position behind the plate. Chuck stands on the pitching rubber and stares in at the myriad of signs Dave flashes, finally nodding his "yes" after a steady headshake of "no." The pitch is a ball. The next iteration of signals and pitch also produces a ball. Chuck takes something off the third pitch, laying it across the middle of the plate. The batter lines a one-hop smash toward second base. Lawrence makes a flailing, self-defense stab at the ball. He rolls, somersaulting, and is shocked to see the ball in his glove. "Holy cow! I got it!" Lawrence shouts as he reaches for the ball in his glove. From his knees he tosses the ball to Trent moving from his shortstop position to the second base bag. Trent bare hands the toss from Lawrence, drags his foot across the bag, and relays the ball to Tony at first base. The four-to-six-to-three double play is turned to perfection capping the Reedville victory.

Chapter 44
Victory

The game is over. Chuck's glove and cap go straight up in the air in a victory toss as the players on the field and from the dugout rush to the mound and join a celebratory dog pile on Chuck. When the mob scene on the mound winds down, Gary finds Chuck. "Congrats. Great job," Gary nods as he extends his hand.

Chuck grips Gary's hand with a simple brief handshake. "You too, buddy," Chuck replies.

All the animosity between the players is washed away in victory. Gary realizes he'll probably never have anything to do with Chuck ever again, and he's fine with burying the hatchet. Gary moves on to find his coach. "Coach Boots, you did it," Gary nods extending his hand.

With a gentlemanly shake of Gary's hand and a slap on the back for his player, Coach Boots corrects Gary. "We did it. The team."

Gary nods and things move from a chaotic celebration to a sense of order as the teams meet at home plate and shake hands. The tear stained streaks are obvious on the dusty, sweaty faces of the Hutton players as they go through the line of handshakes. Most players have regained their composure only to have it broken again as the public address announcer blasts over the speakers, "Ladies and Gentleman! Your 1989 State B Teener Baseball Champions! The Reedville Cardinals!"

It had slipped away from Hutton, and there was nothing they could do. Fate had intervened striking down their ace pitcher. It was no consolation for Alex Chambers. He is unable to speak, and tears stream down his cheeks as he congratulates the Reedville team. He finishes the handshakes with a final grip of Coach Boots' hand. "How's your pitcher?" Coach Boots asks.

Sniffling, Alex nods, "He'll be sore for a couple weeks, but I think he'll recover physically. Mentally...I'm not so sure." Alex laughs uncomfortably, "Look at me. I didn't even play, and I'm a mess."

"Time heals all wounds." Coach Boots smiles. "Just look at me."

The Hutton Coach lets go of Bootsy's hand and acknowledges Bobby Jim as an equal for the first time in his life. "You're right, Coach. Good game. You guys earned it."

Coach Chambers slaps his opponent on the back. The Hutton Bulldogs are called to the center of the ball diamond. The VFW contingent hands out the runner-up trophy and medals.

The Reedville Teeners move to the center of the diamond. Each player's name is called, and he steps forward to accept a trophy. Finally, Coach Boots accepts the championship trophy. Flash bulbs flicker, documenting the historic results of two comebacks never seen before in the history of the State Teener Tourney. Team photos are arranged for parents and fans. Trophies held high, the restless Teeners pose patiently for all photographers, finally being interrupted by the P.A. announcer again. "Your attention please. It is my pleasure to announce the first recipient of the Coach Marvin Willis Memorial Most Valuable Player of the Tournament. This inaugural award is presented to Dave Brown of the Reedville Cardinals. Congratulations, Dave!"

The cheers from the Reedville fans are stoked again by the announcement as Dave steps forward to reluctantly collect another trophy. The fans cheers are outpaced by the players' roar of approval. It is all smiles for the Reedville fans and players. Smiles of joy for the fans and smiles of relief for the players. Gary stands for a few photos with the MVP and his best friend, Dave. Gary's parents and Dave's parents photograph the boys, the last time they will play competitive sports together. Behind the photographers, Gary's eye catches a familiar face. It's Annie and he waves a hand to beckon her over. She jogs over and makes a running leap into Gary's arms. "Uh-oh," Dave groans. "Looks like the picture-taking session is over."

He gives a push to Gary's shoulder and walks away shaking his head.

"I didn't know you were here," Gary beams at his friend as he eases her to the ground.

"Are you kidding?" Annie speaks hoarsely, "I'm sorry. I can barely speak from yelling so much."

Gary hugs her, "That's ok. I'm glad you were here to cheer."

"We closed the café," Annie strains. "Aunt April and I couldn't miss the championship game. Congratulations!"

"Why, thank you. Thank you very much," Gary notes, acknowledging with a slight bow.

Annie bows back and whispers hoarsely, "Thanks for the best summer ever."

Her bow exposes the Saint Christopher medal she wears around her neck. It trickles from her shirt and dangles for a moment before resting on her chest.

Gary reaches for the medallion. He grasps the chain and pulls Annie's face close to his. "I'll never forget it," he whispers in her ear before kissing her lips and hugging her. He holds her tight in the crowd of people. They are surrounded by seventy percent of the Reedville population, temporarily relocated to another small town in South Dakota to enjoy a summer's evening and a victory. From high above, a bird's-eye view would see a swelling mass of humanity under an island of light surrounded by darkness. The midnight celebration is an unduplicated bundle of energy enjoying life in rural America.

Chapter 45
The Spoils

It is Sammy's idea for the bus ride home. Affixed on the hood of the big yellow school bus is the largest, most elaborate hood ornament a bus has ever seen. A few tarp straps and a roll of duct tape fasten the gaudy championship trophy to the hood of the bus.

The players nod approval as they climb aboard the bus, noting the emblem. There is only one question posed by the team: "Who is going to scrape the bugs off the trophy before being placing it in the trophy case at City Hall?"

The answer is: no one. It goes in the case grasshopper guts and all.

The spoils of victory bring another passenger aboard the bus. It is Jeanie. Jeanie is pushing thirty, and her sun bleached hair and blue eyes are particularly attractive. She is a high school teacher and a colleague of Bobby's at Reedville High. Some would even say she is out of Bootsy's league. Sammy was one of those some ones, and he unabashedly reminds his brother that he is in over his head.

Coach Boots, who had rekindled relationship with his girlfriend, Jeanie, saw that she caught a ride down to see the championship game. Now the baseball season is over, she is going to spend some time with Bobby. They had spoken quite a bit by phone since Bobby had been on the road with his minor league team. It is a reconciliation. A compromise is struck, and the young couple seals the deal with a kiss.

It is a long drive home for Sammy. He is left to drive the bus and watch his lovey-dovey brother enjoy a relaxing ride. The music does not suit his taste. He is overcome with embarrassment multiple times at the lyrics he hears in the presence of Jeanie. He does come around a little when the team sings their custom lyrics to Nelson's song "Love and Affection" for the fifteenth time. He joins the chorus:

"I can't live without your
Cock and erection!"

He unconsciously shouts the lyrics, mesmerized by the road and repetitive catchy tune. When he realizes what he has done, he couldn't apologize enough to the lady in his presence. But Jeanie is unphased, "Sammy, I grew up with three older brothers. This is nothin'."

Sammy is finally convinced of the Reedville Teeners' true special musical talents when Warrant's "Cherry Pie" comes on the boom box, and the custom lyrics that Weird Al would envy reverberate through the bus:

"She's my cherry pie,
Smells like fish,
I don't know why!"

Chapter 46
A Quarter Century Later

Over time, the lives of those who played for the Reedville Cardinals Teener Baseball team diverged greatly as is typical of most small towns in the Midwest. The migration of its citizens from the rural communities continues as the dichotomy of job markets evolve and transfer the employment demands from the old agrarian society to an industrial-focused society.

Dave Brown:

At the end of the summer of 1989, Gary and Dave, best friends their entire lives, said their goodbyes on Gary's driveway. "You headin' out?" Dave questioned.
Gary loaded his third suitcase into the trunk of his parent's 1987 Oldsmobile Regency. "Yeah, this is it. My parents are taking a few days off and driving me out to Albuquerque."
"I can't believe it," Dave shakes his head. "You got to be the first person from Reedville to be shipped off to boarding to school."
"Hey," Gary protests. "I chose Kirtland Prep. No one is shipping me anywhere."
Dave extends his arm, and Gary grabs his buddy's hand, pulling him in for a hug. The scene is frozen forever by Gary's mom and her new camera, especially purchased for documenting their trip out to New Mexico.

Dave Brown 25 years later:

Dave Brown made his own way in the world, shunning his guaranteed partnership in his father's successful restaurant business. A Bachelor of Science Degree in Economics at South Dakota State University, followed by an MBA from the University of Minnesota, rounded out Dave's formal education. From there it was a giant leap to Florida to join the merchandising division of Rush Limbaugh's Excellence in Broadcasting, the EIB Network.

Moreover, Dave manages the EIB softball team and can be regularly seen waddling around the base paths of the softball field. He has enjoys a healthy appetite, and his skin-tight Team EIB uniform shirt hugs his enormous frame.

Lawrence Thompson:

After the baseball season, Lawrence resumed his usual hobby…playing pinball at April's Café. His two young female admirers watched him adoringly. The moment is captured forever by "Honey," as Lawrence refers to her. She takes a disposable camera from her purse and snaps a photo of "Sweetie" draped on Lawrence's arm.

Lawrence Thompson 25 years later:

Lawrence Thompson is now a member of the Secret Service. He was recently assigned to President Obama's protection detail. Lawrence can be seen, but barely noticed, in much of the video of the first Black President of the United States. Just look for the inconspicuous, dark-suited, sunglasses-clad agent adjacent to the President.

Yes, Lawrence, there is a Black President.

Aric Carson and Chuck Fisher:

In the Reedville High School parking lot, Chuck and Aric inspect the remnants of the damage to Aric's Camaro. The scuffs and the dings from his run in with the moped ridden by Zach are virtually a memory. Only a person who knew of the crash would recognize the repaired damage. The image is forever frozen with a snapshot from a camera and a candid photograph in the Reedville High School yearbook.

Aric Carson and Chuck Fisher 25 Years Later:

Chuck and Aric became fast friends. Their tight bond leads them to becoming roommates at the University of South Dakota. Aric's father pulled some strings and both were eventually accepted into Wharton School of Business at the University of Pennsylvania. Their journey together continued to New York City. With one helping the other, their teamwork put them in the door as associates in the AIG Investments firm.

In 2009, both men, now in their thirties, were dressed in the finest suits and ties, as they worked frantically shredding documents. Soon, the FBI agents in their blue wind breakers and yellow lettering, broke down the office door. Tossing papers in the air, Aric made a half-hearted break for the exit. It was Aric's meek struggle against his captors that knocked the framed photo of the AIG softball team to the floor, shattering the glass. The economic downturn impacted Aric and Chuck in a significant manner. Convicted of securities fraud, both men were once again roommates in the low-security federal prison located near Williamsport, Pennsylvania. For the duo, their incarceration ironically locked them down just outside the hometown of the Little League World Series.

Annie Willis:

Annie spent the summer in Reedville, learning first-hand about customer service in Aunt April's Café. It was the beginning of a life time of service. April captured the start with a snapshot of Annie in action, coming out of the kitchen with a tray of burgers for delivery to customers in a booth. The beaming, infectious smile of the young woman is frozen forever in the faded photo that still graces her refrigerator.

Annie Willis, M.D. 25 Years Later

Doctor Annie Willis graduated from the University of Minnesota Medical School. She stayed local in her residency as an orthopedic surgeon, and this allowed her to remain an active participant in sports. Not as a player, but as an orthopedic surgeon for the Minnesota sports teams. If you watch closely on Sundays, during the Minnesota Vikings' home games, you'll see Annie on the sidelines as part of the training staff.

Trent Thompson, Turner Jackson, Fin Swenson, and Jesse Ford:

The four farm kids were captured on film at April's Café, sharing a pizza soon after the championship. The photo represents a permanent bond of the young men and the meals they shared that would be repeated as long as they lived.

Trent Thompson, Turner Jackson, Fin Swenson, and Jesse Ford 25 years later:

With the Reedville water tower in the background, Trent, Turner, Fin, and Jesse take a break from their daily grind to play some softball. Each man is now in charge of managing their respective family farms. The wives tend to their children as they watch their spouses relax and blow off steam on the ball field in a friendly softball game. The kids are now in the baseball pipeline themselves, thus assuring the perpetuation of the baseball tradition.

Tony Osmond:

Tony and his family moved to Brayton as he entered his sophomore year of high school. If you review the Reedville year book for that year, you will see the individual photos for the freshmen class. Notice the large, round-faced boy with his eyes closed and smiling. A permanent reminder of the boy nobody would forget.

Tony Osmond 25 Years Later:

Tony began his career at the K-Mart store in Brayton as a part time employee while he was attending Brayton Central High. Now, Tony does a little bit of everything as assistant manager of K-mart. Wearing his K-mart red vest, you can even see Tony rounding up the carts and pushing them toward the front door. It is comical to see the quick-footed, big man run down a stray shopping cart.

A little known fact about Tony is that he has been a successful defendant of three sexual harassment lawsuits against him over his twenty-five years of service to K-mart. It's a mystery why the store keeps him around, but if you see the nearly 400-pound man on the softball team representing the Big K name brand, you'd know he's still nimble on his feet around the bases legging out a double, just as he is in the parking lot wrangling runaway carts.

Coach Bobby Booth:

Coach Boots, as everyone calls him, smiles broadly for the Reedville yearbook photo. The caption reads, "History and Geography teacher Bobby Booth traces the Missouri River on a map of South Dakota."

His career in professional baseball was put permanently behind him by a series of wrist surgeries. The operations on his broken wrist derailed a dream of playing Major League Baseball. Bobby Jim Booth retired from playing the sport he so loved.

Bobby Booth was immediately and fully immersed into the Reedville community. Besides his teaching duties, Bobby was assistant coach for football, basketball, and track. But, his love of baseball remains the same, only from the dugout as a coach.

Coach Booby Booth 25 Years Later:

Coach Boots hasn't changed a bit. Maybe a little heavier and a little grayer, he still coaches Teener baseball in the summer. You can see him arguing with an umpire on the baseball diamonds. He argues, but always with a smile on his face. Oh yeah, he married his long-time girlfriend, and put his own offspring through the Reedville baseball pipeline.

Gary Hillmann:

Gary's mom captured the joy and pain on that summer day with a photo she framed. It was late in the morning when Gary taped the "for sale" sign on the inside of his beloved truck's windshield. The old Ford truck would not be needed at the dorms on the campus of Kirkland Prep in Albuquerque.

Gary Hillmann 25 Years Later:

Gary finished his education at Kirkland Prep, then undergrad at Pepperdine, and finally Pepperdine Law School. At Pepperdine, Gary made his connections and delved into the world of movie production and talent management.

On most mornings you can find Gary in his high rise office in downtown Los Angeles. You'll see him with glass cleaner making sure the front glass doors of "G Mann Productions" are spot-free of fingerprints.

The Teener team photo from the 1989 championship game and the trophy grace his office shelves. Strangely, Gary took the effort to secure the rights to the memorable songs of those long bus rides to baseball games. Rubbing elbows with other Hollywood types has its perks. Warrant provided customized lyrics for their huge hit "Cherry Pie" for Gary. Once in awhile Gary will blast his office with the music of his youth:

> "She's my Cherry Pie,
> Smells like fish
> I don't know why!"

The same with Nelson's hit song, "Love and Affection," Gunnar and Matthew Nelson, the twin sons of Ricky Nelson, had a good laugh when they heard their words tweaked. They went back to the studio and covered their own song with the customized lyrics:

> "I can't live without
> Your cock and erection!"

THE END

Teener Baseball

Greg Heitmann has worked for the Federal Government for nearly 20 years, which pays the bills while pursuing a writing career. His life experiences have been an inspiration for much of his writing. Look for a future book in the vein of one of Greg's writing heroes, Tony Hillerman. Tony Hillerman was a renowned author from Greg's adopted home state of New Mexico. Hillerman penned nearly twenty novels focusing on two Navajo Tribal Policemen. Greg is borrowing this Native American theme, but relocating the geographical setting nearly 1500 miles north and east, to the land of his upbringing, northeast South Dakota and the Sisseton-Wahpeton Indian Reservation. Look for Greg's first novel in this series:

Long Hollow – A Charlie LeBeau Mystery

The novel is expected to be available in December 2014.

www.ingramcontent.com/pod-product-compliance
Lightning Source LLC
Chambersburg PA
CBHW071454040426
42444CB00008B/1326